One Day, All Children . . .

Wendy Kopp

One Day,
All Children . . .

The Unlikely Triumph of

Teach For America

and What I Learned

Along the Way

PublicAffairs

New York

Copyright © 2001, 2003 by Wendy Kopp.
Published in the United States by PublicAffairs™, a member of the Perseus Books Group.
All rights reserved.
Printed in the United States of America.

PublicAffairs books are available at special discounts for bulk purchases in the U.S. by corporations, institutions, and other organizations. For more information, please contact the
Special Markets Department at The Perseus Books Group, 11 Cambridge Center, Cambridge, MA 02142, or call (617) 252-5298.

Proceeds from this book will create a fund to provide grants for corps members to expand
the opportunities available to their students.

Book design by Jenny Dossin.
Set in 11.5-point AGaramond.

LIBRARY OF CONGRESS CATALOGING-IN-PUBLICATION DATA
Kopp, Wendy
One day, all children—: the unlikely triumph of Teach For America and what I learned
along the way / Wendy Kopp. — 1st ed.
p. cm.
ISBN 1-58648-179-7 (pbk.)
1.Teach For America (Project) 2. Kopp, Wendy. 3. Elementary and secondary school
teachers—In-service training—United States. 4. Elementary and secondary school teaching—United States. 5. Education, Elementary and secondary—United States. I. Title
LB1776.2 .K67 2001
372.11'00973—dc21 00-065339   CIP

10 9 8 7 6 5 4

Contents

One day, all children in this nation will have the opportunity to attain an excellent education.

Acknowledgments

My deepest regret as this book goes to press is that I have been unable
to recognize within its pages all those who have been instrumental in
the story it tells. So many people have been a critical part of Teach For
America's growth that it was impossible to include them all. I hope
that even those whose names do not appear in print will read this as
a tribute to their hard work.

I have many people to thank for making this book possible. First
there are those who have been part of Teach For America—our corps
members and alumni, the members of our staff, our advocates in the
education community, our board members and funders, our moral
supporters. You are the reason Teach For America has survived and
thrived. You are the people who taught me the lessons this book re-
counts. I am grateful for your faith, your wisdom, your patience, your
relentlessness.

There are my trusted colleagues who provided invaluable feedback
on drafts of this book: Cami Anderson, Iris Chen, Jerry Hauser, Kaya
Henderson, Kevin Huffman, Dave Levin, Jessica Levin, Daniel Oscar,
Michelle Rhee, Diane Robinson, Abigail Smith, and Neeta Vallab.

There is Kate Darnton, my editor, who has an incredible way with words. Without her intervention, my message would not have been accessible to a broader audience.

There are my parents, who instilled in me the confidence that I could do anything I put my mind to and gave me the opportunity to attain an excellent education.

There is my husband, Richard Barth, who, as you will see, played a significant role in building Teach For America. He has brought me great happiness, and he has put up with my writing this book on our weekends and vacations.

And finally, there are my sons Benjamin and Francis, who now provide new inspiration for the pursuit of our mission.

I feel so lucky to be surrounded by all of you. Thank you for shaping this story and for helping me share it with others.

Preface

As a college senior, I happened upon an idea that would put me in the middle of an incredible movement. The idea was to create a corps of top recent college graduates—people of all academic majors and career interests—who would commit to teach two years in urban and rural public schools and become lifelong leaders dedicated to the goal of educational opportunity for all. Called Teach For America, this corps would mobilize some of the most passionate, dedicated members of my generation to change the fact that where a child is born in the United States does a great deal to determine his or her chances in life.

Schools in America's inner cities and poor rural areas have low academic achievement rates. By the time they are only nine years old, children in low-income areas are already three to four grade levels behind their peers in high-income areas in reading ability. And the gap widens from there, to the point that children born in low-income areas are seven times less likely to graduate from college than their more privileged peers.

As a result, children born in poor communities have fewer life prospects and opportunities than children in the rest of the country. This is not fair. Through Teach For America, my generation is insisting upon educational opportunity for all Americans. To us, this is a civil rights issue.

As the following pages will show, my germ of an idea exploded into a movement. It magnetized thousands of people—including college students, experienced educators, and philanthropists—who shared a commitment to eliminate educational inequality. As a result, Teach For America grew quickly. And it swept me along on a steep learning curve.

I started out as one of the most naive college seniors in the history of Princeton University. That Teach For America came to be in spite of my naïveté is testament to the fact that together idealism and determination can make bold ideas happen.

Of course, it was not easy. Teach For America struggled and nearly died, but thanks to hard work and tough lessons, it has grown into a sustainable, effective organization. The journey has been both illuminating and deeply rewarding.

Along the way, I have met some remarkable teachers and school leaders, people who are fighting with all their might—and succeeding—at putting children in low-income communities on a level playing field with other children. These people have shown me that it is possible to realize our vision. And the fact that it is possible gives us the responsibility—and the opportunity—to make it happen.

I wrote this book about Teach For America's first decade because I wanted to share my journey with others—those committed to eliminating educational inequality, those interested in making their own ideas a reality, and those committed to supporting social entrepreneurs. Please join me in reliving these sometimes difficult, sometimes funny, and certainly instructive ten years.

This book will tell one story of Teach For America. There are thousands of other stories, including those of the individuals who make up our corps, the challenges they've faced, the impact they've had on their students and schools, and the impact their experience has had on them. This is my story—the story of one naive college kid with a big idea.

One Day, All Children . . .

Chapter 1

The Thesis

It was in October of my senior year at Princeton that I realized I needed a plan. What was I going to do after graduation? To this point my life had always been driven toward some academic or extracurricular goal. But now, as I grappled with the biggest decision of my first twenty-one years, I had no idea what I wanted to do. I felt uninspired. I was searching for a place to direct my energy that would give me the kind of significant responsibility that I had enjoyed in various student organizations. I wanted this opportunity right away, not ten or twenty years down the road. More important, I wanted to do something that would make a real difference in the world. I just didn't know what that was.

The issue of my future weighed on me all my waking hours, beginning with my early morning runs. Jogging used to bring me clarity, but now as I ran around the town of Princeton, I felt only more lost. My frustration grew. It became a nagging inner monologue that followed me as I walked across campus between classes or tried to listen to lectures or headed over to Nassau Street, where I would grab lunch and dinner since I'd never found my niche among Princeton's eating clubs. I was in a funk.

This was 1988, and I was a member of the Me Generation. At least that's what the media said. If you believed the pundits, all my generation cared about was making money and leading luxurious lives.

It did seem that just about every Princeton senior was applying to a two-year corporate training program, most with investment banks and management consulting firms. Yet something seemed wrong to me about that "Me Generation" label. Most of the people I knew weren't heading to these two-year programs because they were dead set on making money. Most weren't doing so out of a deep interest in business or high finance either. They just couldn't figure out what else to do. I sensed that I was not alone—that there were thousands of other seniors like me who were searching for jobs that would offer them significance and meaning.

At the same time that I soul-searched about my future, I found myself increasingly engrossed in another issue: the failures of our public education system. This issue had first captured my attention as a college freshman. My roommate, who had attended public school in the South Bronx, was smart and creative. She was a brilliant poet. Still, she struggled under the academic demands of Princeton until she had time to gain the skills necessary to compensate for her weak preparation.

I had attended public schools in an upper-middle-class community in Dallas. My schools had money to spare. A $100,000 scoreboard hung above Highland Park High School's $3 million football stadium with Astroturf that cost $1 million every three years to replace. Our student body was almost completely homogenous, racially as well as socioeconomically. More than 99 percent of the 300 or 400 incoming freshmen would graduate, and about 97 percent would go on to college. Because of the high quality of my schools and the support provided by my family and community, I graduated with an education so solid that I was able to do well at Princeton without locking myself into solitary confinement at the library.

Princeton University was not the most likely place to become concerned about what's wrong in education, but it made me aware of students' unequal access to the kind of educational excellence I had previously taken for granted. I got to know students who had attended public schools in urban areas—thoughtful, smart people—as well as students who had attended the East Coast prep schools. I saw the first group struggle to meet the academic demands of Princeton and the second group refer to it as a "cake walk." Clearly at Princeton I could not glimpse the depths of educational inequity in our country, but the disparities I did see got me thinking. It's really not fair, I thought, that where you're born in our country plays a role in determining your educational prospects.

In an effort to figure out what could be done about this problem, I organized a conference about the issue. At this time I led an organization called the Foundation for Student Communication. Run entirely by Princeton students, it was designed to bring student leaders and business leaders together to discuss pressing social issues. So in November of my senior year, my colleagues and I gathered together fifty students and business leaders from across the country to propose action plans for improving our education system.

There were many interesting discussions and debates, but one in particular stuck out. In a session about teacher quality, nearly all of the student participants—who had been chosen through a rigorous application process and were certainly among the nation's more talented students—said that they would teach in public schools if it were possible for them to do so. And one speaker maintained that people without education degrees were frequently hired by public schools because there weren't enough education majors interested in teaching in low-income communities.

At one point during a discussion group, after hearing yet another student express interest in teaching, I had a sudden idea: *Why didn't this country have a national teacher corps of top recent college graduates who would commit two years to teach in urban and rural public schools?* A teacher corps would provide another option to the two-year corporate training programs and grad schools. It would speak to all of us college seniors who were searching for something meaningful to do with our lives. We would jump at the chance to be part of something that brought thousands of our peers together to address the inequities in our country and to assume immediate and full responsibility for the education of a class of students. I suggested the idea in a discussion group; others responded enthusiastically.

The more I thought about it, the more convinced I became that this simple idea was potentially very powerful. If top recent college graduates devoted two years to teaching in public schools, they could have a real impact on the lives of disadvantaged kids. Because of their energy and commitment, they would be relentless in their efforts to ensure their students achieved. They would throw themselves into their jobs, working investment-banking hours in classrooms instead of skyscrapers on Wall Street. They would question the way things are and fight to do what was right for children.

Beyond influencing children's lives directly, a national teacher corps could produce a change in the very consciousness of our country. The corps members' teaching experiences were bound to

strengthen their commitment to children in low-incom[e]
ties and spur their outrage at the circumstances prev[ent]
children from fulfilling their potential. Many corps members would
decide to stay in the field of education. And those who would go
into other sectors would remain advocates for social change and education reform. They would become business leaders and newspaper
editors, U.S. senators and Supreme Court justices, community leaders and school board members. And, because of their experience
teaching in public schools, they would make decisions that would
change the country for the better.

Now during my morning runs and campus walks, I would roll
the idea of the teacher corps over and over in my head. This could
be huge, I thought. This could be the Peace Corps of the 1990s:
Thousands would join, and, in the long run, we would fundamentally
impact our country.

As I became increasingly excited about the idea of a national
teacher corps, I was still trying to figure out a practical answer to my
own uninspired job search. Teaching just might be it, I thought. I
went to the career services office. They referred me to the teacher
preparation office, which helped ten to twenty Princeton students attain teacher licensure each year. It was too late for me to enter this
program, but the office pointed me to a file cabinet stuffed with job
applications and certification requirements from school districts across
the country. The files were a mess of mismatched, multicolored, jar-
gon-filled papers.

Overwhelmed by all the information and completely confused
about whether I could actually teach without an education degree, I
decided to call the New York City public schools directly. I spoke with
a former teacher who was working to recruit recent graduates of East

Coast colleges to teach in New York. He told me that if I could wait until Labor Day, I would probably get a teaching job. The schools couldn't be sure of their job openings until then. This was a major disappointment. I needed money to live on right away, and I wanted greater certainty—for my sake and my parents—that I would actually have a job after graduation.

This whole experience was discouraging, and it only made me more convinced of the need for a teacher corps that would recruit as aggressively as the investment banks and management consulting firms that were still swarming all over campus. The teacher corps would make teaching in low-income communities an attractive choice for top grads by surrounding it with an aura of status and selectivity, streamlining the process of applying for teaching positions, and assuring recent graduates a job and a steady income despite districts' inability to hire them until Labor Day.

I became so obsessed by the idea that I decided to try to make it happen. I wrote a letter to President George Bush suggesting that he should create this new corps. John Kennedy had set up the Peace Corps, I thought. Who better than the President of the United States to create the teacher corps? With high hopes, I mailed off an impassioned letter. It must have slipped into the wrong stack. In return I received a form letter rejecting my application for a job.

At some point in December, I saw that I simply needed a job—a job that would pay my bills after graduation. So I made a weak attempt, applying for a total of five positions—one at an investment bank, two at consulting firms, one at a food products company, and one at a commercial real estate venture.

And I began musing about another possibility. If the President wasn't going to create a teacher corps, maybe I could start one as a nonprofit organization. My experience at the Foundation for Student Communication, where I managed a staff of sixty and sold hundreds of thousands of dollars' worth of magazine advertisements and conference sponsorships, made me think that I just might be able to pull this off. More important, I didn't have the experience to see why it couldn't be done.

Meanwhile, as a senior at Princeton, I was obligated to write a thesis. I had been looking for a topic that would inspire me to spend hours and hours researching and writing. After the education conference, I knew that the teacher corps idea was my answer. Here was something that motivated me personally and that would also satisfy my requirements at the Woodrow Wilson School, Princeton's public policy program.

And so, during the spring of my senior year, I withdrew from the world—skipping whatever classes I could and talking to just about no one—in order to research the viability of a national teacher corps. I was certain such a corps must already exist somewhere—it was too obvious!—or that there was some reason it wouldn't work.

I couldn't find one. Just as the conference speaker had told us, even in times of general teacher surplus there is always a shortage of qualified teachers in very low-income areas, and it is possible for individuals who haven't majored in education to be hired to meet the need. And although there were a number of initiatives to improve the recruitment of new teachers, there was no national teacher corps. I also researched potential models—the Peace Corps, the teacher corps that had been run by the federal government in the 1960s, and alternative certification programs that existed in certain states to ease people without traditional teacher certification into teaching.

As I wrote my thesis, I became all the more determined to make

ty. I thought it would have such power, in the short run
...g run. Thankfully, the firms to which I was applying
for more conventional jobs made my choice easy. I didn't get a single
offer. I remember standing at a pay phone at school, hearing the Morgan Stanley recruiter—my last remaining corporate possibility—tell
me that they had decided I wasn't the right fit for the firm. I was upset
by this rejection, but I figured it must have happened for a good reason. The moment I hung up, I made my decision. I would start the
teacher corps.

In the end, I produced "A Plan and Argument for the Creation of a
National Teacher Corps," which looked at the educational needs in
urban and rural areas, the growing idealism and spirit of service
among college students, and the interest of the philanthropic sector
in improving education. The thesis presented an ambitious plan: In
our first year, the corps would inspire thousands of graduating college
seniors to apply. We would then select, train, and place five hundred
of them as teachers in five or six urban and rural areas across the country. According to the budget calculations I had done, this would cost
approximately $2.5 million.

I knew we had to start big. Only a monumental launch would convey the urgency and national importance of our effort. And only that
would inspire the nation's most talented graduating seniors—those
with the most attractive career options—to forgo other opportunities
to be part of this movement. I found support for this plan in my research about the Peace Corps. President Kennedy had appointed Sargent Shriver to develop a proposal for the Peace Corps, and most of
Shriver's advisers suggested a cautious beginning. But Shriver knew
that a corps that proceeded gradually would never become a symbol of
the New Frontier. And so Shriver recommended that Kennedy create

the Peace Corps by executive order, that it be launched within weeks, and that several hundred volunteers be placed within the year. Shriver's plan led thousands of idealistic college students to apply, and it ensured the Peace Corps's place as an enduring part of the American landscape. His theory worked for the Peace Corps. I was sure it would work for the teacher corps.

In early April of 1989, a week before my thesis was due, I called Marvin Bressler, then chairman of Princeton's sociology department. Professor Bressler had agreed to be my thesis adviser on the condition that I make an argument for mandatory national service. I accepted the condition because, as the last senior in my department to decide on a thesis topic, I didn't have much choice. I had tried to convince Professor Bressler of what I thought to be the brilliance of my idea, but he said I couldn't write a thesis on something that amounted to little more than an advertising campaign for teachers. I was banking on Professor Bressler's forgetting his stipulation. So instead of telling him what I was really writing about, I steered clear of him until the last minute.

When I finally called Professor Bressler one week before the due date, I wasn't sure if he would even remember agreeing to be my adviser. So I reminded him that I was the student proposing a national teacher corps and then told him that I had completed a draft of the thesis. "I've actually decided to start the corps," I told him. He suggested I drop the draft off. I did. Two days later he called to ask me to stop by his office.

I walked across campus, terrified of what this brilliant, opinionated man would think of my paper and, more than anything, worried that he might insist I revise it. Would he force me to make a pitch for mandatory national service?

Professor Bressler quickly put my fears to rest. What he really wanted to know, he said in his booming voice, was how in the world I planned to raise the $2.5 million. I told him I was positive Ross Perot would help. Having grown up in Dallas when Mr. Perot had led a campaign to improve Texas schools, I was certain he would love my idea. And given his own background, surely he would relate to something so entrepreneurial. "He's from Dallas, and I'm from Dallas, and he's really into education reform," I said.

Professor Bressler leaned back, contemplating my answer. He didn't seem convinced. "Do you know how hard it is to raise twenty-five *hundred* dollars?" he asked. He arranged for me to meet with Princeton's director of development, who could fill me in on just how difficult it would be.

Chapter 2

Suspending the Laws
of the Universe

On April 12, 1989, the day after I turned in my thesis, I went back to the computer room to turn it into a thirty-page proposal. I was excited to be moving forward but anxious about what needed to be done in the less than two months before graduation. I needed a seed grant so I could survive after college with no other source of income and so I could spend my summer traveling around the country meeting with education leaders, school districts, and as many potential funders as possible. Without a grant, I would have to get a real job and there would be no teacher corps.

So I went to Princeton's library. This time I wasn't searching for volumes about the state of education or the history of the Peace Corps but for a reference book. I needed the names and addresses of the chief executive officers of major American corporations. I picked companies I recognized and also those that had surfaced in my thesis research as being committed to education reform.

Within a week, I had photocopied my proposal, stapled a red card stock cover on top, and sent it off to Ross Perot and the CEOs of thirty companies such as Mobil Oil, Delta Airlines, and Coca-Cola. In each packet I enclosed a letter requesting a meeting to discuss how the company might be able to help me with my plan. Then I started calling to follow up on the letters.

I didn't get through directly to the CEOs, but my letter did make its way down various corporate ladders, and I got meetings with six or seven executives. It didn't occur to me to be surprised that I was securing any meetings at all. Instead I mostly just wondered why the CEOs themselves didn't think this idea was worthy of their time. But I was happy to have any audience, so while my classmates spent April and May unwinding from our thesis ordeal and celebrating our imminent graduation, I dressed up in suits and took New Jersey Transit into New York for one appointment after another. More than once, as I struggled out of bed to catch the 6:30 A.M. train into the city, I wondered why I hadn't chosen a normal path.

That May I met with executives at Xerox, IBM, AT&T, Metropolitan Life, and New Jersey's Dodge Foundation. I also met with an official in the Department of Education; the dean of Harvard's undergraduate teacher education program; the head of the Education Commission of the States, which advises states in their efforts to improve education; and Stanley Kaplan, the founder of the test preparation company and a man deeply committed to education reform.

Everywhere I went, I described my idea and why it had to happen. I talked about the impact a national teacher corps would have and why it would work—how all around me college students were searching for a way to assume a significant responsibility and make a difference, and how they would jump at the chance to act on their ideals. I described my plan and why there had to be at least five hundred corps members the first year. And then I explained what I was looking for: a seed grant and $2.5 million within the first year. I wasn't feigning confidence; I really *was* confident. I was sure that the plan would work and that it would work in exactly this way. Looking back, it seems somewhat astounding that anyone would take me seriously. But at the time I didn't see any reason for these funders to doubt me.

One of my letters landed in the hands of several executives at Union Carbide, which had just formed a task force to explore how their company could contribute to education reform. One afternoon I got a call in my dorm room. An executive from Union Carbide told me that he and another task force member would be in New Jersey the next day. Could they take me to lunch? I was excited and nervous with anticipation: Anyone interested enough to take me to lunch was bound to help me. The next afternoon not only did I get a free salad at a fancy restaurant off campus, but I was offered office space in Manhattan and an introduction to Union Carbide's CEO.

This was good, I thought, but not good enough. What I really needed was a seed grant. Although I was doing everything I could think of, I was running out of time. Still, I didn't develop an alternative plan. Something just had to work out. This was an idea that simply had to happen.

Another letter landed on the desk of Rex Adams, Mobil's vice president of administration. Mr. Adams agreed to meet with me. Throughout the meeting, he kept asking, "What are you going to *live* on?" And I kept responding, "That's exactly why I need a grant." At the end of our meeting, he suggested I send him a budget. I put some ambitious numbers down on a sheet of paper, held my breath, and mailed it to him. Less than a month before I graduated I got word that Mobil would be offering me a seed grant of $26,000.

My organization was not incorporated, let alone granted tax-exempt status. So on Mr. Adams's advice, I decided to ask Princeton University to act as my conduit of funds. I called the director of development I had met just weeks before at Professor Bressler's suggestion. He must have been shocked. I phoned him at about 6:00 P.M. He checked with Princeton's general counsel, and I got a call back that night confirming that the university would be happy to act in this capacity.

Getting Started

I graduated in June. After the ceremony, my parents drove me to New York City. I was nervous about what lay ahead. Would I be able to convince enough people to support my plan? But I was also elated to be on my own finally, without classes and without anything to distract me from my mission. And I was thrilled to be moving to New York City, where I had yearned to live ever since my first visit to Manhattan during my freshman year.

My parents dropped me off at a brownstone on West Seventy-eighth Street, where I would share an apartment with two other women. I had found the place on a bulletin board. It cost $500 a month, which wasn't bad for New York City at the time. I hauled my belongings—three trash bags of clothes and a sleeping bag—to the second floor. The apartment had four rooms with tall ceilings and hardwood floors; mine was a tiny room in the back with white-painted brick walls. It was perfect. After laying out the sleeping bag and stacking my clothes in organized piles, I left to wander the streets. I quickly discovered Café La Fortuna, a dark coffee shop a few blocks away on Seventy-first Street. I was in heaven.

The next day I made my first trip to my donated office in a sky-scraper at Forty-fourth and Madison. There I would work, all alone, from nine in the morning until well after midnight all summer long. It was somewhat lonely; the only people in the building who knew I existed were two clerical staff who worked for Union Carbide and seemed completely uninterested in why I had invaded their space and the evening security guards, who would inquire sympathetically about why I was working so hard. Yet as lonely as it was, I loved the inde-pendence. In a letter home to my parents in the middle of June, I ex-pressed my sense of freedom: "I just love living like this," I wrote. "I love looking at a calendar and seeing that tomorrow is blank and just deciding what to do with it."

My summer goal was to meet as many potential funders as I could, convince them of my idea, secure start-up grants, talk with educators who could help me refine the plan, and generally test its feasibility. There were the legal issues of setting up a nonprofit corporation, but those were soon taken over by Union Carbide's lawyers. And there was also the challenge of settling on a name. I considered a few options and landed upon "Teach America," which I felt captured the national importance of the endeavor. As it turned out, a medical company had already laid claim to that name. In the fall I would spend hours trying to come up with an alternative. One night on the subway in Washington, D.C., where I had gone for a day of meetings, it struck me that the answer was as simple as inserting an extra word. Thus, we became Teach For America—even better than Teach America, I thought, in that it was a call to action and communicated a sense of service.

In pursuit of as many meetings as possible, I would spend days in the office sending out hundreds of letters and making hundreds of phone calls, generally with limited results. At times things got a little depressing, but I persisted because I was just certain that my message would ultimately get through to enough people. And there were breakthroughs. One day Roby Harrington, an executive at Young & Rubicam who had been involved in the first Peace Corps advertising campaign, called me and said, "Wendy, I just read your proposal. It's stunning. Let's meet tomorrow." That single phone call kept me going for a week.

As few and far between as those types of calls were in that first summer, it's amazing how much encouragement I did receive. Here I was, a twenty-two-year-old with $26,000, a donated office, and a plan that within twelve months I would have five hundred corps members in training. How incredible that experienced executives, seasoned enough to know that this was an unrealistic scheme, would even listen to me! Alden Dunham, the program chair of education at the Carnegie Corporation, sent me a positive letter. "My suggestion is that you come down the street and we could chat further about what appears to be a very worthwhile undertaking," he wrote on June 27, 1989. "As a former dean of admissions at Princeton and as the guy who has helped to stimulate much of the concern about teachers in this country today . . . I am delighted to see that another Princetonian is taking the lead in trying to get at a very difficult problem." Harold McGraw Jr., who since retiring from McGraw-Hill had spent a great deal of time working on literacy issues, called and said he had read my letter and was impressed by it. Jennifer Eplett, a recent graduate of Harvard Business School, called out of the blue to say that she was working for a new foundation that had heard about what I was doing and wanted to work with me. It turned out that she was helping to start the Echoing Green Foundation, which invested in "social entrepreneurs" and would become a strong force in the development of Teach For America.

Other interactions were less encouraging. Many people could not accept that a young woman with no real-world experience could possibly run such an ambitious, untested enterprise.

"Who's going to *run* this?" asked a foundation officer in a major insurance company. I told her we would have between five and ten recent college graduates working around the clock. "You know, let me tell you something," she responded. "That's just not going to work. I mean, people need defined job assignments and goals." Now, looking back, I can see the wisdom in her counsel. But at the time I thought it was the most shortsighted, nonvisionary, bureaucratic advice imaginable. I was not discouraged.

The CEO of Union Carbide also had his doubts but offered his support anyway. "You know, Wendy, most people who do these things are professional administrators with lots of experience. This is a big job," he said. Yet he agreed to join our advisory board and write letters of introduction that would get me through the door to Vernon Jordan and the chief executives of several major companies committed to education reform.

When I asked for $100,000 from Union Carbide's foundation, however, I ran up against an obstacle I would later encounter again and again: The person heading the company's education task force believed Teach For America ran counter to conventional thought about what needed to be done to fundamentally improve teaching. I was baffled. How could Teach For America do anything but raise teaching standards? We were talking about recruiting the most talented graduates in the country to teach. Where was the conflict?

I learned that the dominant belief held that teachers, just like doctors and lawyers, needed to be trained in campus-based graduate programs before entering the classroom. From this vantage point, the only acceptable way to improve teaching was to ensure that schools of education raise their selection standards and make their programs more rigorous. Proponents of this view were reluctant to invest in Teach For America, whose recruits would go through only a short pre-service training program before entering the classroom.

Beyond the fear about our corps members' receiving inadequate teacher education, there was another concern. Although some educators were eager to encourage new talent to enter teaching in our lowest-income communities, others were worried about the negative effect that such young people, unfamiliar with the communities in which they would be working, could have. In one case I met with a highly regarded urban school superintendent. As I explained my plan, he became very upset, indeed downright angry. He told me I was wasting his time, that he didn't need more do-gooders teaching in his district. His reaction, which was more fervent and heartfelt than any of the skepticism or naysaying I had heard before, reduced me to tears. I tried to hold myself together when I was in his office, but once I got into my rental car, I broke down completely.

I had a similar encounter with another gentleman—a foundation head and longtime advocate for children in low-income communities—who had agreed to meet with me for the express purpose of counseling me out of my enterprise. He was concerned that despite the corps members' good intentions, two years in the classroom wouldn't be enough to do any good. Worse still, he thought our teachers would simply add to the unpredictability of their students' lives. He said that after "finding themselves," our inexperienced, privileged teachers would leave their kids feeling abandoned.

What these two men told me had an impact. I thought and thought about their concerns. Ultimately, their counsel heightened my awareness of the challenges inherent in what we were doing. But I felt they were underestimating the commitment and humility of the recent graduates who would join the corps. These would be caring people who would go above and beyond to meet their students' needs and who would be driven to learn from their students, their students' families, and their colleagues. I was sure these qualities would enable corps members to have a significant impact in the lives of their students during the years they taught them, and also that many corps members would be pulled into a lifetime of teaching and working in low-income communities.

I was also determined that we would be a diverse group; we would include college graduates from privileged backgrounds and middle-class backgrounds and people who had grown up in the kinds of communities where we would be working. I felt we needed to make a particular effort to recruit individuals who shared the socioeconomic and racial backgrounds of their students and thus would bring a vital perspective to our corps and organization. At the same time, I felt we needed to recruit as broadly as possible, since students needed as many teachers as possible who were talented and driven to help them reach high expectations. Moreover, as I thought about our goal of influencing future leaders, I knew our corps would need to be reflective of our future leadership—inclusive of people from low-income communities and also inclusive of people from more privileged communities.

One thing that inspired me to persist was the enthusiastic response I received from most school districts. I remember one visit in particular, to the personnel director of the Los Angeles Unified School District. When he looked over the list of colleges where we were planning to recruit, he laughed out loud. "You'll never get people from these colleges to teach here," he said. "You think someone from Stanford is going to want to teach here? I'll tell you what: If you can get them, we'll hire them. We'll hire all five hundred of them!"

So that first summer after college took me all across the country at a crazy, exhausting clip. In Boston I met a number of nonprofit leaders, including Alan Khazei and Michael Brown, who upon graduating from Harvard Law School the year before had cofounded an urban service corps called City-Year and who would provide much support and guidance from that point forward. In Michigan I met executives from the Kellogg Foundation, the foundations of the big three automobile companies, and a couple of education reform organizations. In Washington I spent some time gauging the interest of the D.C. public schools and talking with people who had led the federal teacher corps of the 1960s. (That corps, which started with a mission similar to that of Teach For America, evolved dramatically so that it did not resemble our model by the time it was eliminated by the Reagan administration.) I also traveled all over California and to Chicago, Pittsburgh, Rochester, and cities in New Jersey and Connecticut, talking with all the potential funders, educators, and school system officials who would meet with me.

Almost everyone advised me to start smaller: I should recruit fifty people for one site, learn from that experience, and then expand from there. But this perspective was counter to my very conception of what

Teach For America would be. This was not going to be a little non-profit organization or a model teacher-training program. This was going to be a *movement*.

Through my travels I assembled my first board of directors. I asked a few people—social entrepreneurs and educators—who shared my enthusiasm for the idea. They were Jim Clark, who had started AC-CESS, an organization dedicated to helping people find employment in the nonprofit sector; Rick Belding, who had started Recruiting New Teachers, an initiative to get people into teaching through advertising campaigns; Jennifer Eplett, who had helped start City-Year and then worked for the Echoing Green Foundation; Sue Otterbourg, a consultant active in education reform; and Wayne Meisel, who had started COOL, the campus-based organization that recruits young people into volunteerism. At the same time I assembled a board of advisers composed mostly of the corporate chiefs whom I had met through the head of Union Carbide.

I also managed to secure a new donated office, one big enough to accommodate the staff members I planned to hire that year. I asked for this space in a meeting with Richard Fisher, the CEO of Morgan Stanley, who may have agreed to meet with me because he was also a Princeton alum. Recognizing the irony of my request, I asked for prime office space from the same company that had decided not to hire me just a few months before. I doubt that Mr. Fisher knew what he was getting into when he agreed to house us on a pro bono basis, pay for our phone service, and let us use Morgan Stanley's print room for free. This arrangement proved invaluable over the next five years; by the end of our time there, when our national staff numbered forty people, our chief financial officer estimated Morgan Stanley's gift was saving us at least $500,000 a year.

. . .

When September rolled around, I was utterly convinced that the national teacher corps made perfect sense. Many people agreed. They just didn't believe that thousands of outstanding college graduates would join. The most common concern I'd heard all summer was that college students would not want to teach in public schools in low-income areas. Yet this was one thing I had absolutely no doubt about. I was sure my peers would want to be part of something this important, that they would give anything for this opportunity. Because this was exactly the area where I had the greatest confidence, I decided to move forward and launch an ambitious recruitment effort. Once Teach For America succeeded in inspiring thousands to apply, I figured, the skeptics would be won over, school districts would hire our teachers, and funders would give us the money we needed. Such certainty was the benefit of inexperience.

Building Our Team

That fall I was ready to move ahead full force. I decided to hire four people—one to manage the recruitment and selection of corps members, another to design and organize the summer training institute, a third to manage the placement of corps members into teaching positions, and a fourth to help with overall administration. I was terrified of bringing on these additional staff members. Wouldn't they question why I was in a position to manage them? But there didn't seem to be any other option.

I didn't figure that anyone but other recent college graduates would be willing to take a risk on an untested idea. Neither did it seem that seasoned people would roll with the less conventional aspects of my plan, like the idea of starting out with thousands of applicants and hundreds of corps members, or the idea of moving forward without any money in the bank. So I set out to find some other young people to work with me.

One day in late August, I was back at Princeton for meetings with potential supporters when I ran into the director of Princeton in Asia, a program that sends Princeton grads to teach in Asia for a year. The director asked me to stay and attend a dinner for the students who had just returned from their year abroad. I sat through the dinner wondering why I was there. When asked to address the group, I said no more than a few sentences about what I was trying to do with Teach For America. Immediately after I finished, Daniel Oscar, one of the teachers who had returned from China, ran over to introduce himself. With great urgency he said that he wanted to talk more about Teach For America and would be happy to drive me back to New York. All the way up the New Jersey Turnpike, Daniel interrogated me about my plan. By the time we reached Manhattan, he had announced that he wanted to work with me part time. He was taking Chinese at Columbia and looking for something to do on the side. I told him I needed to think about it. Two days later I received a five-page memo from him outlining why he should work with me.

We got together at a sandwich shop near my office. Our meeting was tense; having never hired anyone before, I had no idea what I was supposed to do. Daniel, who had a mop of curly brown hair on top of his wiry frame, seemed as uncomfortable as I was. He's an intense person, and it seemed that he really, really wanted to help make Teach For America happen. Because he only wanted a part-time position, I figured I had nothing to lose. So over a Diet Coke, without even the pretense of an interview, I agreed to take him on as my first employee.

It turned out to be one of the best decisions I made. Not only is Daniel an immensely responsible person, but he is one of the most brilliant thinkers I've ever met. He would play a significant role in shaping the way we thought about everything from selecting and training our corps members to office technology and compensation structures.

Daniel was the first to come on board, but he wasn't the first person I had hired. Back at Princeton I had offered a position to a friend of my younger brother's. Whitney Tilson was a Harvard grad who was sitting on a job offer from the Boston Consulting Group. He had other obligations for the summer but wanted to join me in the fall. I couldn't believe that someone from Harvard would give up a great career option to take part in my effort without even meeting me.

Whitney finally showed up in October, a very blond, very tan guy with a large smile and a lot of energy. He started managing the administrative and financial matters that were beginning to pile up. A few days into his tenure he produced a memo showing exactly how little money would soon be left of Mobil's original $26,000. I already knew we were running low on cash. I was counting on potential funders to come through with additional grants to make it possible to pay the salaries of my new team. Each of us was to make $25,000—which seemed appropriate since it was slightly less than the first-year teacher salary in New York.

Kim Smith, a 1989 graduate of Columbia University, was the next person to join our team. She had several years of part-time and summer experience working on business-education partnerships with Sue Otterbourg, the educational consultant who had agreed to become a member of our first board. I met Kim during one of my meetings with Sue, and she struck me as smart and spunky. Education and teaching were in her blood—her dad was a professor of education at Teachers College—and she agreed to take charge of designing and organizing the summer training institute.

Our start-up team was rounded out by Susan Short, a Stanford graduate who had just finished her two years of service in the Peace Corps. She had seen a job announcement I had run in the Peace Corps newsletter for returned volunteers. Susan was a tall, quiet, thoughtful woman, with two years of real-world experience at that. She assumed responsibility for finding the teaching placements for our recruits.

By October the five of us had moved into our new digs, courtesy of Morgan Stanley, on the thirty-third floor of the McGraw-Hill building at 1221 Avenue of the Americas, in the heart of midtown Manhattan. The space was nothing fancy—it was a shell of white, scratched-up walls and gray industrial carpet that showed the wear and tear of previous tenants—but it seemed positively palatial to us. One of my first nights in the office, well after midnight, I stacked together some red, white, and blue wire in/out boxes to serve as staff mailboxes. We scrounged some mismatched donated desks and chairs and took over four of the offices on the otherwise empty floor. I set myself up in a small room with no windows in the middle of our space. This would be the national headquarters of our powerful movement.

No sooner were we settled than I realized we would need more people. Other recent graduates had heard about our effort, through Daniel or Kim or the potential funders I was meeting, and they would come in to see me. If they seemed enthusiastic about our mission, I would offer them rather undefined jobs.

In November I mounted a search for people who would travel around the country beginning in February to interview the thousands of people I expected would apply to Teach For America. I had written the chairman of Hertz a letter over the summer, and he had agreed to donate six rental cars for this purpose. My hiring criteria were simple: I was looking for a dynamic and racially diverse group of people capable of inspiring college students to join the cause.

I found twelve people who fit the bill. Two in particular would end up playing a significant role in Teach For America's development: Ian Huschle and Richard Barth. Ian had graduated from Harvard in 1988 and had spent a year teaching in Tangier. Upon his return, he had joined a prominent New York law firm as a paralegal. He complained so bitterly to a friend of my roommate's about the boredom of his position that she suggested he call me to see if he could volunteer. After a brief meeting, I realized we needed Ian. He struck me as exceedingly thoughtful, and there was no doubt in my mind that his outgoing personality and striking presence would enhance our reputation on college campuses. Ian's classic good looks were so impressive that literally every member of our small team came into my office after he left and asked, "Who was *that*, and what was he doing *here?*" Ian wasn't actually seeking a full-time job, but I offered him one anyway. He ultimately accepted.

Richard stopped into the office one day for an impromptu interview. His mother had sent him a *New York Times* column about our fledgling effort while he was traveling in Europe after graduating from

Harvard that June. I was so overwhelmed with work that I only allocated about ten minutes to our discussion. Richard seemed smart and personable, but I wasn't sure we could use another preppy white guy from an Ivy League college on our small team. Lisa Bornstein, another new hire, knew Richard from Harvard. After he left, she told me that he needed to know right away whether he had a job or not. I gave it about fifteen seconds of thought—since it was all I had to spare—and said that we would have to say no. She never conveyed the message to Richard, and a week later, when I began to panic about not having enough recruiters, she placed a yellow adhesive note with Richard's number on my desk. He came on board.

Meeting the Magic Number

Within two weeks, Daniel's part-time job had turned into thirteen-hour days. His responsibility was to inspire college students to apply to Teach For America. Our strategy was to identify two student leaders to be our "campus representatives" at each of one hundred colleges. We selected public and private schools from all over the country on the basis of their academic competitiveness and ethnic and racial diversity. There were small and large campuses, historically black colleges and Ivy League schools. We planned to bring the two hundred campus reps together at a conference in December and then rely on them to spread the word about Teach For America through grassroots strategies. We found the representatives by calling friends and friends of friends and contacting student organizations and deans of student affairs. To ensure the diversity of the group, we aimed to find one rep and then have that person find another rep who was from a different racial background.

TEACH AMERICA
P.O. Box 5114
New York, NY 10185
October 23, 1989

Dear College Student,

I enjoyed talking to you on the phone about TEACH AMERICA.

We know, contrary to what the media would have us believe, that today's students are as willing as ever to "give something back" to America. Perhaps what lacks is a common spirit, a common mission. And yet our nation faces a number of internal threats that call for the help of our brightest young minds. Foremost among them is the dilapidated state of our educational system.

You have probably heard the statistics—that 700,000 students drop out of high school *each year,* and 25 percent of all our children never finish high school, that students in the United States score below those of almost all other industrialized nations in science and math, that only 25 percent of 17-year-olds are able to write what the National Assessment of Educational Progress terms an "adequate" persuasive or analytic essay. One thing on which business and government leaders from different industries and political parties agree is that the state of the educational system is threatening America's future.

Pages 30–32: This was the first letter Daniel Oscar sent (before we changed our name to Teach *For* America) in the effort to recruit campus representatives.

We are a group of recent graduates who believe that today's brightest, most motivated students of every race and academic major should join together to help the United States in the places they are most needed—the schools. Therefore, we passed up jobs in management consulting and investment banking and Senator's offices to create TEACH AMERICA.

TEACH AMERICA will use the Peace Corps model—lots of publicity, a selective application process, active recruitment—to attract top recent graduates, train them, and place them as teachers in inner cities and rural areas which suffer from persistent teacher shortages. Recruits will commit to two years in teaching.

The success of TEACH AMERICA relies on our ability to develop a broad base of student support. That is why I am writing to you. In order to develop that essential network, we are targeting one committed individual on each of 100 college campuses to serve as our "link" to that school. As Campus Representative, you will create TEACH AMERICA "YOUR COLLEGE." Your organization will work to ensure widespread campus awareness of the problems in education and of the need for teachers and will help in TEACH AMERICA recruitment efforts. On the evening of December 1, TEACH AMERICA will fly each of the campus representatives from the 100 schools to Princeton University where we will all sit down together to brainstorm how best to publicize on campus the frightening state of our schools and incredible need for teachers.

Almost thirty years ago, an enthusiastic group of college students pushed for the creation of an organization that would enable them to serve the United States by furthering the development of non-industrialized nations. Today, as a result of those students' efforts, thousands of America's brightest, most motivated graduates travel abroad to serve in the Peace Corps.

With your help, we can assemble a similar group of people—the graduates with the most other career opportunities—to TEACH AMERICA, and to help improve our own dilapidated schools.

Because our Campus Representative conference begins on December 1, time is very short. Our team of campus representatives must be assembled by November 11. Please read the enclosed booklet and return the enclosed information sheet so it is in our office no later than November 3. If you have any questions, please don't hesitate to call me at 212-974-2456.

Sincerely,

Daniel Oscar

P.S. If you want to be the Campus Representative but are unable to return the information sheet by the necessary date, please call our office *immediately* so we can make alternative arrangements.

P.P.S. If you are not able to be the Campus Representative for your college, but agree that our schools are in dire need of teachers, please do your best to find someone else on your campus who you think would do an absolutely amazing job as Campus Representative. One quick look at your calendar shows that we do not have a lot of time left and so I am relying on people like yourself to help TEACH AMERICA build the Campus Representative team by finding a committed individual on your campus to take on the job. If your friends are unavailable, your Dean of Students or Dean of Minority Affairs might be a good person to suggest qualified students. I cannot stress enough how big a difference you can make in the TEACH AMERICA effort by bringing to our attention a person determined to help make a difference.

The fall was not easy. As exciting as it was that many college students were signing on to advance our mission, we faced several crises before the December conference arrived. First, we weren't anywhere near our goal of two hundred campus representatives. I decided to pull our four staff members from whatever they were doing so we could all focus on recruitment. To make things worse, we didn't have enough money to buy the plane tickets to get the two hundred representatives to Princeton, which had agreed to host the conference for free. Thankfully, a friend of Daniel's family who was a travel executive with connections at American Express got us a $70,000 line of credit.

On December 1, 1989, after a week of all-nighters by our small team, about two hundred campus representatives descended upon the Princeton campus. I should have been excited—this was the first clear sign that a greater movement would actually develop out of the initial idea—but I was too exhausted to even think about celebrating. I should have been terrified, too.

On the first morning, I stood at a podium for two and a half hours, answering dozens of questions that the reps fired at me in an unplanned session. They were searching for details that had not yet been resolved. Where would people actually teach? When would the summer training start? Where would it be? What exactly would happen there? Would corps members be able to choose where they taught? How would the corps members and their belongings get to their teaching sites? Where would they stay until they found a place to live? When would they get their first paycheck? How would they get cars if they didn't already have them? How would we decide what subjects they would teach? What kind of support would we be providing once they assumed their positions?

Knowing that we needed to inspire their confidence, I did the best I could. I came up with answers and delivered them with resolve, as though they'd been decided months before. I'm not sure I succeeded completely, but most of the reps seemed fired up by the end of the weekend. "Imagine how you all will feel next summer when hundreds of top graduates are in training for Teach For America," I said in my closing speech. The group stood and cheered.

The conference generated quite a bit of momentum. Fred Hechinger wrote a column about our efforts in the *New York Times,* and *Newsweek* ran a two-page piece. We had called a few major media outlets and told them what was going on, and they sent reporters out to cover this display of idealism from the Me Generation.

Moreover, there were indications that our recruitment strategy was working. Jonathan Snyder, one of our representatives at Yale, wrote flyers and slid them under the door of every senior on campus several days before school let out for winter break. Within three days Jonathan had received 170 calls on his answering machine. Later in January, the representative at Carleton College called to say that 100 of the school's 450 seniors had showed up at an information session.

As soon as the campus representative conference was over, Ian began developing the selection criteria and interview process for new corps members. Beyond ensuring that our first corps members were up to the challenge, our goal was to appear selective. We needed to counteract teaching's image as a "soft" and downwardly mobile career. So Ian developed a tough interview with a number of potential teaching scenarios and pointed questions to gauge each candidate's persistence and commitment. It was the following question, though, that may have done more than any other to shape our image on campus:

(1) What is wind? Don't describe it, just tell me what it is. (2) Phenomenologists draw an analogy between religion and the wind, claiming that one can't see religion, only the manifestations of it—like synagogues, churches and mosques. Similarly, one can't see the wind, only manifestations of it—waves in a wheat field, moving branches. What's another analogy you can draw to the wind?

Looking back, I have to laugh at the thought of our recruiters asking this question of every applicant. But it created the desired effect. Teach For America was clearly not something for the intellectually meek.

The interview was complemented with an essay application and a five-minute sample teaching session in which candidates were asked to teach other candidates on a topic of their choice. Daniel had learned this strategy during his time working at the test-prep company, The Princeton Review.

Through these selection tools, the recruiters would identify candidates who, based on twelve criteria, were either "exceptional" or "outstanding" on a six-point scale. Some of our staff had researched possible selection criteria by interviewing school principals and reading books and articles on the subject. Then we refined the criteria through night after night of intense staff debates. The twelve desired characteristics, which we carefully defined (and have refined over time), were persistence, commitment, integrity, flexibility, oral communication skills, enthusiasm, sensitivity, independence and assertiveness, ability to work within an organization, possession of self-evaluative skills, ability to operate without student approval, and conceptual ability/intellect.

While Ian worked away at the process for selecting corps members.

SOMETHING TO THINK ABOUT

December 6, 1989

Dear Yalies:

Teach For America is a national effort beginning this year to attract talented graduating Seniors to teach for two years (regular pay) in schools which most need teachers in New York City, Washington D.C., Chicago, Los Angeles, Indian reservations in New Mexico, the Rio Grande Valley in Texas, rural areas in North Carolina, Louisiana, and inner cities in New Jersey. Begun by a Princeton student, it has brought together an unprecedented combination of student talent, teachers, non-profit heads, and corporate CEOs. Due to this combination of idealism, experience, clout, and funding, *Teach For America* has great chances for success. It relies on only one thing—the most important factor of all: YOU.

Do you have the least bit of indecision about your plans after graduation? Would you consider devoting two years to teach for America, in either elementary or high school grades, to make her a continuously competitive nation, one capable of continued sustenance of her democratic institutions, with equal opportunity for all? Math and science majors—remember that America has been steadily sliding in her technical and scientific capability.

Pages 36–37: This is the front page of the flyer our campus representatives at Yale distributed to college seniors. The back page was a copy of the *New York Times* column about Teach For America. A total of 170 students responded to this flyer within three days.

People of color, recall that perhaps the single greatest key to achieving full equality lies in achieving high levels of education. Liberal arts majors, remember that America is headed towards dangerously low levels of literacy, at precisely the time that they need to be high. Yalies, remember the great privilege we've been given, and please consider, before embarking on your ambitious careers, to devote two years towards bolstering the general strength and well-being of our nation.

If you find this interesting, no matter what year you are in, just call 436-0740 and leave your name, number, year, and interest on the machine. *It's important that you call before the break.* There is no obligation; this is just so that we can get you more complete information before break. In any event, think about it–talk about it, with your parents and friends, and feel free to call and ask questions.

Sincerely,

The *Teach For America* Reps, Yale

Jonathan Snyder   Melanie Moore
JE '90   MC '90

Teach For America   *Teach For America*   *Teach For America*

Richard began helping to coordinate the efforts of the campus representatives. Almost immediately he came back with a handwritten memo stating the absolute improbability that we would meet our goal of 7,500 applicants. With some simple math, the memo showed the level of interest that would have to exist on each of our 100 campuses in order to meet the goal compared to the level of interest indicated by the evidence we had. Richard was clearly right. But what could we do? In response to the memo, Daniel stepped up our efforts to motivate the reps. I crossed my fingers.

Our twelve recruiters went on the road, two to a rental car: Sonnet Retman and Ian Huschle, Richard Barth and Guilaine Jean-Pierre, Bruce Baker and Sonja Brookins, Allison Jernow and Paul Hagan, Kim Smith and José Calero, Michael Gilligan and Joelle Fontaine. Excited about their mission but anxious about the gravity of their task, they fanned out to their assigned regions with a map and the phone numbers of each of our reps and the career service office contacts who had been collecting applications. Each night they called in to tell us about campuses where we were flooded with applicants and campuses where there were none, about how well or how poorly they were getting along with their recruiting partners, about getting lost in their travels.

With the recruiters on the road, I was left back in New York with about eight new hires who helped answer phones, plan the summer training institute, and hunt down teaching positions for our recruits. We quickly realized that we had no system to process the applications that the recruiters sent back to the office. The result was chaos. Acceptance and rejection letters were two months late.

Along with everything else, I soon found myself trying to develop a scientific method for matching applicants' site preferences and qualifications to districts' requirements and needs. The work was piling up. My solution was to begin sleeping every other night.

Daniel captured the extent of the crisis in a memo that he distributed to our staff.

Teach For America: The Crisis

More than a month ago we were at Reed College. We have yet to enter the applications into the computer. More than two weeks ago we were at Georgia Tech. We have yet to receive the applications from the interview team. More than 6 weeks ago we were at Yale. Yesterday we finally informed all of the 68 applicants of their status. We promised two weeks in all of our promotional material. We are barely responding within 6. Investment banks, management consulting firms, private schools are busy wining and dining their recruits; we are unable to even call ours. Every hour phone calls come into this office from angry applicants wanting to know their status. We cannot respond.

After months of unprecedented labor by all of us, everything we have done may disintegrate in the next 30 days. The scariest part is that the crisis continues to loom and we are wandering aimlessly among the thick fog of impending failure. Our intensity of two weeks ago and last week has waned, but the crisis only garners strength and flourishes. Its depth is far greater than I can imagine. We are falling further and further behind, not catching up. . . . We do not know to whom we have sent letters and to whom we need to send letters. We have stacks of incomplete applications sent in by our interviewers. We have received 16 commitments, but have no matriculation packets to send them. We are on a path which is leading us to an empty training institute, empty classrooms, and a non-existent teacher corps.

What we need now is immediate action, energy and stamina. Our last two weeks of intensity must only intensify until we have finally eliminated this threat to all that we have done. . . .

The people most directly involved with this crisis need to meet immediately to come up with a plan to get us out of this crisis immediately. We need to figure out how we can most effectively utilize all the resources available, and we need to become scared. Very very scared.

–Daniel

As it turned out, we did not have 7,500 applicants, but thankfully, we had miscalculated on another score: The quality of applicants was higher than we expected. From the 2,500 applicants, we easily chose 500 great candidates.

The Mysterious Source of Our Confidence

The recruitment and selection effort was only one of many challenges. We also had to design and organize an eight-week training institute for five hundred new teachers and find school systems in five or six areas across the country that would commit to hiring the teachers sight unseen. And even more daunting, there was the challenge of raising the funds to pay for all this.

It seems something of a miracle that I maintained my confidence throughout that first year. Why didn't I crumble under the stress or the workload? Why didn't I despair that we would never get the applicants we needed, that we wouldn't convince school districts to hire our teachers, that we wouldn't raise the necessary funds? I think it was a blind faith in the power of the idea that kept me going. I'm not sure that the prospect of failure was real to me, although there were a few moments when it crept into my mind.

I was worried when the Echoing Green Foundation found a graduate student to write his thesis about Teach For America. Of all the potential anxieties I could have, it was this poor guy I was concerned about. What would he do if our plans fell apart? I also remember sitting in front of an office computer at two or three in the morning, trying to imagine what it would be like if five hundred college graduates actually showed up at the summer training institute we were planning. At that moment it didn't seem possible. What was I thinking? But these moments of doubt were few and far between. More often, I took for granted that if we worked hard enough, our plan would work. It simply had to. This country *needed* a national teacher corps.

What's amazing is that I was surrounded by others who felt this same sense of sheer confidence. Richard wrote me the following note during his recruitment tour:

3/25/90

Dear Wendy,

It's two in the morning and Guilaine and I are now safely tucked away in the Baltimore Best Western. Guilaine is presently immersed in a deep sleep, and so I am forced to stare at the hideous powder blue walls that surround me. . . .

What a fantastic group of people I got to meet at Georgetown. And at all the schools for that matter. I can't tell you how exciting it is to meet these people, and to see how much they want to make a difference. To contribute in some positive way to our nation's future.

Even on the days when I've had little sleep, and dread asking the same questions, I can't help but be energized. So many people want to be a part of Teach For America, and their excitement is fantastically contagious.

I guess I just wanted to tell you how glad I am to be a part of this program. Of this team. I *know* we have a winning combination. I *know* we are going to succeed. I just wish you could see all the amazing people I'm meeting as we move up the coast.

It was funny tonight when we talked on the phone. I asked how you were doing, and you said, "You mean how is fundraising going?" I wasn't thinking about fundraising when I asked you that question, but the fact that you brought it up made me realize how much weight must be on your shoulders.

Well, for what it's worth, I want you to know that I am also 100% confident that we are going to raise the money. (I doubt that you really need any assurances.) It's going to be tough, but I know you and I know our staff. *Nothing* is impossible.

Take care,

Richard

Raising $2.5 Million

My approach to fundraising—beyond sending several unanswered letters to Ross Perot—was to continue writing hundreds of letters to corporations, foundations, and wealthy people. Most of these letters seemed to disappear into a big black hole, despite persistent follow-up calls.

For the hundreds of meetings I didn't get, however, I found a few people who decided to invest in our idea. Alden Dunham at the Carnegie Corporation, the Princeton alum who had written me during the first summer, sent me another letter exactly one year later committing $300,000 toward our goal. Jack Mawdsley, the director of education programs at the Kellogg Foundation, later told me he didn't really believe I could pull off such a feat but was so taken by the concept and my conviction that he invested $40,000 and a great deal more in credibility. Robin Hogen, the vice president of public affairs at Merck & Company, told me over the phone that he wanted to be our first major corporate sponsor before I ever met him.

We gained some recognition in the funding community. *Fortune* magazine was focusing heavily on the business sector's involvement in education, and I remember a reporter calling and saying that she had received six letters from corporations suggesting she cover us. "Why is this such a hit?" she asked. Part of the answer, I think, was timing. The failures of our public education system had begun to receive national attention. Blue-ribbon commissions were reporting on the extent of the problem, and companies were just beginning to search for education reform initiatives they could support. But they hadn't been searching long enough to latch onto a different big idea.

Still, I was becoming extremely worried. We weren't enough of a hit. As of April 1990, we had inspired 2,500 people to apply to Teach For America, selected 500 of them to join the corps, begun organizing the institute, and convinced school districts in six sites to hire our corps members. Yet I had not raised even half a million dollars toward our goal.

Then one day a staff member yelled down the hall of our makeshift national office, "Wendy! Ross Perot is on the phone." I assumed the caller was a friend of mine playing some kind of sad joke, but in fact it was Ross Perot. My heart was thundering. I could hardly breathe, let

October 17, 1989

TEACH AMERICA, Inc.
P.O. Box 5114
New York, NY 10185
(212) 974-2456

Dear Chief Executive,

I graduated from Princeton this past June and have been working to put my
senior thesis into action ever since. I proposed the creation of an organization that would use the Peace Corps model—active recruitment on a national
scale, a selective application process, lots of publicity, a short initial time
commitment, and a centralized application, training, and placement mecha-
nism—to attract top recent graduates into teaching in the United States.
With the help of a number of business and education leaders, I have created
the organization as a privately funded non-profit called TEACH AMERICA,
Inc. I am writing to request your help.

Currently, a "development team" of five of us is working to create a national
recruitment effort, to construct a unique summer-long training institute, and
to attain commitments from school districts in five major inner-city and rural
areas to hire TEACH AMERICA recruits. Our Board of Advisers, still being
compiled, includes: David Kearns, chairman & CEO of Xerox; Robert
Kennedy, chairman & CEO of Union Carbide; Tom Payzant, superintendent

Pages 44–45: This was one of the letters I wrote to funding prospects in the
fall of 1989.

of the San Diego School District; Felice Schwartz, president of Catalyst; and George Sella, chairman & CEO of American Cyanamid. Initial financial and in-kind support from Mobil, Union Carbide, Morgan Stanley, Young & Rubicam, American Cyanamid, Apple Computer, and General Atlantic Partners has made possible our activities to date.

Our vision is that teaching becomes the "thing to do" on college campuses, that thousands of top graduating non-education majors decide to commit themselves to teaching; that they mitigate the persistent teacher shortages which exist in our inner cities and rural areas; and that thousands of incredibly sharp individuals, whether they remain in teaching or enter business or government or law, will have the knowledge and commitment to be spokespersons for teacher professionalization and educational reform.

We're certainly a lot closer than we were three months ago, but we will need a lot of help between now and next September if we are to see our vision become reality. I would love to meet with you to discuss TEACH AMERICA, to hear any ideas and input you might have, and to talk about how you might be able to help us in the effort. I will call your office shortly.

Sincerely,

Wendy Kopp

alone speak. I told him that I would be in Dallas the following week and asked if we could meet. He agreed. I got off the phone and scheduled a trip to Dallas.

I have never ever been so determined in a meeting in my life. I knew that I had no option but to leave Ross Perot's office with the funding necessary to train and place our corps members. Before I walked into his office, I formed an image in my head: I would stay firmly glued to my chair until I had a commitment. I was terrified—not by the prospect of meeting Ross Perot but by the thought that Teach For America's fate rested on the success of this one meeting.

I entered Mr. Perot's ornate office and sat down on what I remember to be a red leather couch. I must have explained my mission, but all I remember is Mr. Perot talking. He talked a lot, and I had trouble following much of what he was saying. I was mostly just thinking, "I need to stay here until I get $1 million from this man." When Mr. Perot suggested that I contact Sam Walton and other philanthropists instead, I insisted that he himself was the best possible prospect. Finally, after two hours of back and forth, Mr. Perot agreed to offer us a challenge grant of $500,000. We would have to match his money three to one. I'm not sure what ultimately led Mr. Perot to this idea. He must have realized that I wasn't planning to go anywhere until he committed to something. Or perhaps he felt that he had nothing to lose. His grant proved to be the catalyst we needed: Other donors (some who had been skeptics and others who were just waiting for a sign that additional funding would come together) came through with the remaining $1.5 million in relatively short order.

I left Mr. Perot's office, charged to the nearest pay phone, and called Daniel. Before I could open my mouth, Daniel started in, frustrated that I was off in Texas while he was pulling all-nighters trying to process applications. After listening for ten minutes, I told him Ross Perot had made a challenge grant of $500,000. "That's just great," Daniel told me, and then he hung up. As I would see many times in the coming years, the stress and chaos of an enterprise like ours meant that real accomplishments were rarely adequately celebrated. We were all too busy grappling with the next challenge.

Exactly one year and ten days after I graduated from college, 500 teacher corps members gathered in the University of Southern California's auditorium for the opening ceremony of Teach For America's first summer training institute. They were some of the country's most sought-after recent college graduates. They came from a diverse group of 100 colleges. Twenty-nine of the corps members came from Yale, with the other colleges most represented being Tufts, Princeton, the University of Wisconsin, Vanderbilt, Harvard, SUNY Binghamton, Cornell, Brown, and the University of Michigan. They were unified in a collective commitment to increase the opportunities available to kids in low-income areas. There was an electrifying energy in the room. It had happened. This was exactly what I had envisioned. I could hardly believe we had finally reached this day.

The media caught on to what was transpiring. "Princeton Student's Brainstorm: A Peace Corps to Train Teachers," read the headline on the front page of the *New York Times* on June 20, 1990. Two days later *Good Morning America* followed with a feature. Several weeks later *Time* magazine printed a page-long article.

For years, whenever I was asked how I had accomplished this feat, I would reply that there was nothing magical about it. I simply developed a plan and moved forward step by step. Teach For America came together because the idea was good and the plan made sense. But now I see that this answer is insufficient. I once heard that when an idea is meant to happen, the laws of the universe are suspended to make way for it. When I look back over the first year of Teach For America, it's clear to me that had something to do with it. Here was evidence that even the most idealistic visions can come to be.

Chapter 3

When Idealism Isn't Enough

The momentum was more than I had bargained for. It all came to a head at the training institute. A few months prior, we had gathered an advisory group of talented practicing teachers and professors in the teacher training field. We asked them to determine the shape of the institute and the design of the curriculum. According to their plan, corps members would student teach in the mornings. In the afternoons they would receive guidance and instruction from a faculty of teachers and teacher educators.

We decided to bring the inaugural Teach For America corps members to Los Angeles because the year-round school system could accommodate an influx of student teachers. We formed an agreement with the University of Southern California to use their facilities. And we selected the faculty through telephone interviews of candidates who had responded to advertisements run in education publications. Everything seemed to be in place. But it was too much.

Eight Long Weeks

At the institute opening ceremony, I found myself surrounded by corps members who were clapping and chanting "TFA . . . TFA . . . TFA." There was something disconcerting to me about this spontaneous enthusiasm. Perhaps I was wise enough to know that there's a very thin line between exuberance and disillusionment. I must have sensed that if the corps members were more level-headed at the outset, they would be more level-headed when confronting the tremendous challenges in their classrooms. And they might be more understanding when faced with the disorganization of a young and inexperienced Teach For America.

In fact, it took less than one week for corps members to plummet the short distance to disillusionment. I soon found myself in the middle of a crisis.

We had made a couple of poor selection decisions. One corps member in particular terrorized our staff and corps so much that he had to be removed from campus by security—though not before he had time to call Ross Perot (who took his call) and report that Teach For America was engaging in "distinctly anti-American activities."

There were also much larger problems. Some corps members criticized each other for their lack of sensitivity and awareness. Some questioned whether corps members coming from positions of privilege had the perspective, humility, and self-awareness to become effective teachers. Tensions were so high that lectures escalated into free-for-alls. Corps members took the mike to offer their perspectives, attack fellow corps members, and usually harass the guest lecturer as well.

Corps members' frustration with Teach For America was only amplified by organizational snafus. Early in the summer we learned that there was an error in our application materials. In a section of our brochure describing a federal program that offered loan forgiveness to teachers in low-income areas, we didn't explain that the provision did not apply to individuals graduating before 1991—all of our corps members. Within a week we did what we thought we had to do; we promised that Teach For America would itself forgive the loans. This would cost our financially strapped organization more than $100,000. Still, that pledge was not enough to win back the lost confidence.

Things were made even more difficult by our spartan accommodations. One of our money-saving strategies was to pack corps members into rooms in far greater numbers than intended by the dorms' architects. Another was to avoid the expensive USC food service at breakfast by serving our own bagels and cream cheese. Two of our college interns would drive a van at 4:30 in the morning to a local bagel supplier. By 5 A.M. five hundred bagels and slabs of cream cheese were set up on picnic tables in the courtyard for corps members to grab before their morning teaching assignments.

Perhaps the biggest issue of all was that the institute design was so loose. Our instructions to faculty members, whom we had not even met prior to the institute, consisted of a page-long list of the topics they were expected to cover and the themes they should reinforce. Thus the quality of the training varied widely depending on the faculty member. Some corps members felt blessed to have hours of advice from extremely talented veteran teachers. Other corps members became extremely frustrated with sessions they felt were unproductive. Given the circumstances, it was extraordinary that the faculty hung in there at all. I think they fed off the energy of our corps members and the idealism of our concept. They certainly could not have been impressed by the sparse guidance we provided them.

While I worked behind the scenes to tackle all the issues that cropped up, I also withdrew into my shell. I'm not a people person by nature, and my shyness was accentuated by the fact that our smart, demanding corps members terrified me. I tried to be as invisible as possible. We had set up temporary offices in a suite of dorm rooms, and I would go there very early in the morning and stay there until very late at night. It got to the point where I feared even going to the cafeteria.

After the longest eight weeks of my short life, the corps members finally left. But not before Ray Owens, who will forever be remembered by his 488 fellow corps members, reminded us of the reason we had all come together in the first place. He had been selected to deliver the corps member speech at the institute's closing ceremony. What he said moved me deeply:

It is with a good deal of reservation and humility that I stand before you, my colleagues, TFA staff, faculty, family, and friends. . . .

Far too many of the children we will encounter have decided that the American dream is an eternal nightmare. The monsters of educational failure have locked them into the dismal dens of ignorance and despair. They have internalized the low level of expectation and inferiority that many of this nation's school systems have designed and perpetuated for them. America has said to these children that their dreams must be deferred. . . . The nation that promises "liberty and justice for all" has failed these children by sending them to schools that don't offer courses in calculus and literary analysis, courses that they will need in order to prepare for the demanding course-work of our institutions of higher learning. The country where "all men [and women] are created equal" has said to these children that they are an exception to this rule by consistently allowing unequal educational opportunities to exist between the haves and the have-nots. . . .

In these classrooms it will not matter that you are a Phi Beta Kappa. The children in Compton or rural Georgia may not be impressed that you attended a prestigious university. When the school bell rings at the close of the day, it will not matter whether you graduated magna cum laude or "thank you laudy." . . . What will matter will be your ability to earn the respect and admiration of your students. These children need our genuine compassion and respect. That means that we will have to show them that we care and that we believe in them. . . . Saying it will just not be enough. We must show it in the way we look at them. . . . We must show it in the way that we encourage them. . . . And we must show it in the way that we work relentlessly in their behalf. . . .

We should believe that we have as much to learn from our students as they have to learn from us. Each one of them has an experience. . . . Each one of them has a story. We must learn that experience and listen to that story. For, embodied in these stories—embedded in these experiences—is the history of our nation and our world. Sometimes it will tell an unpleasant story. But it is one that we must contend with. Sometimes it will tell the story of the brutal boot of oppression that has trampled the culture and spirit of many marginalized groups in our country. Yet, until we face these truths, until we face these children, we can never begin to eradicate the wrongs that still exist. . . .

I leave this institute with fresh hope . . . a hope that is rooted in a belief that when people care enough and believe enough that they really can make a difference. I challenge you to care. . . . I challenge you to believe today. There is a little girl in Baton Rouge who needs to know that you care. There is a little boy down in Compton who needs to know that you believe in him. We must all realize our vested interest in this project. Whatever our differences may be, now we must come together on the issue of providing the best possible education to the young people of this nation.

When the school bell rings on day one and all our students are in their seats, we will hold the future of this nation and this world in our hands. Whatever we do will have lasting implications, not only on the lives of those students, but also on the lives of all those who they come in contact with. So then, the question that we should ask ourselves should not be, "How can I make this work?" The question must be, "How can I afford not to make this work?"

The day after the institute ended, our corps members dispersed to their classrooms in New York City, Los Angeles, New Orleans, Baton Rouge, and rural areas in North Carolina and Georgia. And then the school bells rang and Teach For America's first year really began.

Our Debut in the Classroom

As corps members headed out to do the real work of Teach For America, I was relieved to return to New York after an exhausting summer. I still felt responsible for guiding our mission forward, but it was wonderful to have my personal space back. Once again I could peacefully buy my lunch at a deli instead of an institutional cafeteria, where I might face an onslaught of angry complaints. I could go on my 6 A.M. run around Central Park without fearing that corps members might see me while on their way to their morning teaching assignments. And I was glad the institute was over. It was (relative) bliss.

I had put Richard Barth in charge of placing corps members and finding support for them. He had hired a regional director in each site—a person to set up a local office, work with school districts to ensure corps members were hired, and coordinate a local support network of regular meetings and newsletters. Some of the regional directors were hired in May, others as late as July. All of them were, again, recent college graduates. Who else would be daring enough to accept such a challenge?

Despite the districts' earlier agreements to hire corps members, it soon became clear that actually securing the teaching positions was another matter. In some cases unexpected budget cuts reduced the number of available teaching posts; in other cases school principals had already hired other teachers by the time our corps members arrived for interviews. Understandably, these situations only increased corps members' frustration and decreased their confidence in us. But thanks to around-the-clock efforts by Richard and the regional directors, our corps members did end up in teaching jobs—though some not until a few weeks into the school year, after other new teachers had resigned their positions or student enrollment numbers had settled.

A couple of weeks after the summer institute, I went to visit our corps members in rural Georgia. This trip was exactly what I needed. In the classrooms of Wheeler and other nearby counties, I saw what I had envisioned when I dreamed up Teach For America: bright, enthusiastic corps members who inspired their students and impressed their principals and colleagues. As I walked into one school, three experienced teachers stopped me in the hall to say thank-you—"Thank you so much for bringing them here. It's so wonderful to know that such bright young men will teach in our school."

The principal in this school had tried to disband the classroom of Tarik Lemtouni, one of our corps members, when it became clear that enrollment numbers would be lower than predicted. The principal told me that he reversed his decision when the students threatened to stage a sit-in if they were forced to move to another teacher.

In another school the assistant superintendent took me around to see our corps members in action. After stopping in one Spanish class, he said, "Did you see that? Those kids were engaged. I've never seen our kids engaged in a Spanish class." All this, and our corps members had been teaching only two weeks. They were still sleeping on each other's floors.

But as the school year progressed, problems arose that I hadn't foreseen. In October, New Orleans teachers went on strike. Our anxious corps members weren't sure what to do: Should they strike with their fellow teachers or cross the picket lines? And if they went on strike, would Teach For America support them financially, since they had yet to receive a single paycheck? Meanwhile, in New York, the city threatened major budget cuts by midyear, requiring the school system to lay off thousands of teachers on a last hired, first fired basis. Suddenly our corps members were worried about losing their jobs.

And everywhere corps members were finding that teaching was very, very hard work. Their experience student teaching in the classrooms of master teachers in Los Angeles hardly prepared them for what they now faced. It was one thing to student teach in the classroom of a veteran teacher and quite another to create a well-managed classroom from scratch. Now corps members shouldered the full responsibility of planning whole days of effective instruction day after day, helping students overcome the myriad obstacles that kept them from focusing on academics, and coping with paperwork demands and administrative politics. All of our corps members—regardless of their socioeconomic and racial backgrounds—faced steep learning curves as they sought to understand the values, dreams, and customs of their particular students.

Corps members found themselves for the most part in new and un-
known communities, grappling with the most challenging teaching situations in America. They told us that we hadn't set accurate
expectations, that we hadn't given them adequate training, that we
weren't providing sufficient professional development.

Unfailing Sense of Possibility

Even with all the issues that had cropped up, I somehow maintained
my initial optimism. After all, despite the rough spots, things had generally worked out so far. Whatever the skeptics said, we had in fact
placed five hundred corps members in schools across the country and
we had raised the $2.5 million we needed. It seemed to me that any-
thing was possible. I kept thinking big.

In our first year I had started bringing together the entire staff for
Monday night meetings. These strategy sessions would begin at about
9 P.M. We would order Chinese take-out and cram together on my living room floor; once the group grew too large, we took over an empty
end of our thirty-third-floor office space, which we called "the room
with a view." The space, which would now rent for about $100 a
square foot, had floor-to-ceiling windows overlooking the Manhattan
skyline. Our meetings generally ended at two or three in the morning.
Finally, sometime during the second year, I reluctantly agreed to implement a rule that all staff meetings would end by midnight.

In one of the first Monday night meetings after our return to New
York, we discussed the issue of scale. Many people thought we should
stick to 500 new corps members per year. But I felt we needed to grow
dramatically in order to convey the power of our movement. So I ar-

gued for recruiting 1,000 corps members in year two. We must have
spent dozens of hours in heated debate over this issue. We couldn't
agree, and I didn't want to compromise on an issue I thought was so
fundamental to our mission. Finally, frustrated that others didn't share
my sense of possibility, I made the call.

Beyond expanding the scale of Teach For America, I was determined to improve our effectiveness. We needed to refine our selection
model, strengthen the summer institute, and build a system for supporting corps members after they began teaching.

Our caffeine-fueled Monday night sessions led to a spate of fresh efforts. We searched for five new placement sites to accommodate a
larger corps and a full-time staff of recruiters who could present a
more professional image than our current group of volunteer representatives. We also planned to interview potential institute faculty in
person, train them before the institute began, and create a more manageable training structure. We developed plans to support our corps
members in the field. We planned a conference for our corps members
between their first and second years. And we decided to bring our op-
eration into the 1990s by networking our offices, providing each staff
member with a computer, and building sophisticated databases.

Of course these ambitious plans would cost more money—$5 mil-
lion, twice as much as we raised for our first year. But the plans were
necessary to fulfill our mission, so I thought we had no choice. We
simply had to find the money.

As it turned out, I had underestimated the challenge of meeting our
new recruitment goal. As we entered the spring, it became clear that
we would receive only about 3,000 applications. About 700 applicants
would meet our selection criteria. We'd be 300 short.

This didn't squelch my spirit, however. By this time I had shifted my focus from ensuring we met our recruitment goals to ensuring our teachers received the training and support they needed. At first, when we got wind of the challenges our corps members were experiencing, we dispatched staff members from our lean national office to New York and Los Angeles, our biggest placement sites, to go on school visits and staff the local offices. To boost morale, we held holiday parties and sent greeting cards with encouraging words. But this was clearly inadequate.

Corps members were not getting the guidance and professional development they needed from their schools, and the local universities in which many had enrolled to meet certification requirements had not generally tailored their programs to meet the needs of beginning teachers in low-income areas. Corps members demanded more. And our board members and funders did, too. As they heard reports from the field, they told me that it was Teach For America's responsibility to provide our teachers with more support.

I was easily convinced. I wanted to do everything we could to guarantee corps members' success. We began hiring experienced teachers to help corps members in their professional development. These support directors, who would work out of our local offices, would spend their time visiting corps members in their classrooms and giving them advice.

As each month passed, we added to this strategy. We realized that one support director couldn't be responsible for 100–200 new teachers, so we hired more. We realized that corps members needed more than sporadic classroom visits, so we began offering workshops and bringing corps members together for small group discussions. Missing our goal of 1,000 corps members saved us money, but providing corps members with more support increased costs. Our year-two expenses would come in at $5 million. In year three they would be $7 million.

Raising the Money

I spent most of my time trying to raise funds. I figured the amount of money raised would be a direct function of how much energy we put into it, not of the capacity and priorities of the funders. The harder we worked, the more financially secure we would be.

Ian Huschle volunteered to help. Having secured a few grants for a club at Harvard, he had more fundraising experience than anyone else. I was grateful to have his assistance. We continued the approach that had worked in the first year, writing hundreds of letters requesting meetings, making follow-up calls, visiting potential funders, and following up diligently with the contacts we made. We traveled all across the country meeting with corporate executives, foundation officers, and potential individual donors. We went to the areas where our corps members were teaching and to other places where we thought we would find sources of funding and people interested in education reform.

We succeeded in generating meetings with some of the nation's leading executives. In our second year, we met with Steve Jobs, founder of Apple Computer, as well as John Scully, its CEO at the time. We met with Dick Munro, former CEO of Time; Robert Crandall, CEO of American Airlines; Ed Donley, CEO of Air Products and Chemicals; Richard Rosenberg, CEO of Bank of America; Clarence Smith, CEO of Essence Communications; David Kearns, CEO of Xerox; Les Alberthal, CEO of Electronic Data Systems; and Bob

Wycoff, CEO of Arco. We met with financier Henry Kravis and with Hillary Clinton. (Her husband had sent us a one-sentence letter saying we were needed in the Mississippi Delta, and she advised us on how to expand into the area.)

Why did we enjoy this level of access? In part, I suppose, it was because we were bold enough to ask for it. By now we also had an impressive board of advisers, a dramatic one-year track record, and lots of media coverage. At the time we thought it was perfectly normal to have meetings with such important business leaders. We weren't particularly excited about these opportunities; mostly we were just exhausted. Our fundraising trips involved numerous and often delayed flights and days crammed with appointments in one corporate office after another, where we would repeat the same spiel. We spent our nights in dreary motels.

Unfortunately, my personality wasn't exactly suited for a rigorous schedule of speeches and presentations. In October 1990 I had an interview on *Good Morning America*. As she scanned my pale face, the makeup person said, "Oh, dear. We have to wake you up." I thought to myself that I was wide awake; it was just that I didn't know how to chitchat with this stranger. But if we were going to meet our big goals, I would need to play the extrovert, and so I forced myself to learn how to be more effective in these situations. During fundraising meetings, I analyzed how Ian managed to make conversation so effortlessly. How did he think of all those things to talk about? How was he so at ease with all these people he'd never met?

Ian and I never knew how we would pay the bills more than two months into the future. Every week we would shudder at the dwindling sums in Teach For America's bank account and double our resolve to make dozens more calls and schedule more meetings. Every week we would secure the necessary money just in the nick of time. This grew increasingly stressful—all of Teach For America was depending on us to keep the money coming.

Keeping Things Together

It was a lot for me to balance. I was always involved in fundraising meetings or staff meetings or writing memos about how to improve our program or writing letters to funders or making phone calls or reading through the growing stack that filled my in-box on a daily basis. There was little room to breathe. I might find a couple of hours a week to go to a movie or eat dinner with my roommate, and I reserved an hour a day for my morning run, but other than that I was entirely consumed by Teach For America.

My travel schedule was crazy. During the first five months of our second year, I took twenty-five trips, crisscrossing the country from New York to Los Angeles, Miami to the Bay Area.

Here's how I spent one typical week in October 1990. I took the red-eye from Los Angeles to New York Friday night, landed at 7 A.M. Saturday morning, had brunch with a Teach For America evaluator at 10 A.M., and then interviewed potential staffers every hour on the hour between 12 and 6. Ian and I then flew to D.C. on Sunday for an interview with *USA Today* and a conference about education organized by *Fortune* magazine. Monday night I flew back to New York City for our weekly Monday night meeting. Tuesday I went to New Orleans to attend a reception for Teach For America. I stayed in Louisiana through Thursday, attending meetings in New Orleans and

Baton Rouge. Friday I was off to Austin, Texas, for our second conference of campus representatives, and I finally returned to New York City on Sunday. I had to do all this before I had figured out that I should hire an assistant and before modern-day conveniences like voicemail made it easy to communicate with people from the road.

Each day—actually, every few hours—was filled with extreme highs and lows. Take the Monday in June 1991 when I left a business conference about education in Washington, D.C., to meet with an angry principal in New York City. Members of the school community had seen an article that we had sent to potential applicants; it quoted a corps member describing the community in derogatory ways. The corps member had been misquoted, and we should never have mailed the article out. I wanted to apologize to the principal and look for ways to defuse the charged situation. My plane was delayed, and I was worried about the signal my tardiness would send to the principal. Thankfully the meeting was delayed as well, and I arrived before it started. Here I was, a white twenty-three-year-old who had never been in front of a classroom, trying to dispel tension among veteran African American teachers and administrators more than twice my age. Hoping that sincerity would get me through, I plunged in. I was only partly successful. The corps member kept her job, but my apology wasn't accepted. I missed my flight back to the conference in Washington; the plane I finally boarded was extremely late. Again I was frustrated, this time at missing the opportunity to meet potential funders, but I arrived back just in time to hear the last few sentences of the keynote speech by IBM's CEO, John Akers. One of our supporters introduced me to him after the dinner was over. Mr. Akers told me that he had been trying to convince his daughter to apply to Teach For America. "How amazing is this?" I thought to myself. "The CEO of

IBM actually knows about Teach For America, and on top of that he wants his daughter to join!" I returned to my motel that night, spinning from the ups and downs of my day.

In addition to taking me on an emotional roller-coaster ride, my fundraising schedule shuttled me between two strikingly different economic spheres: our underresourced classrooms and the plush world of American philanthropy. That June I made a trip to California. One day I visited Compton High, one of the most problem-ridden schools in Los Angeles. I walked around an ancient two-story school building; paint was peeling off the walls, and the hallways were dark. Seven corps members were teaching in the school. One of them, Mark Swinton, had converted an old auditorium that was being used as a storage room into a theater. His students performed elaborate productions that attracted hundreds of community members.

After our school visits, Ian and I had dinner at a fancy restaurant with Dick Riordan (who would become mayor of Los Angeles), Rick Guerin (a highly successful businessman), and Jackie Cotsen (former head of strategic planning for Citicorp and then the wife of Lloyd Cotsen, the head of Neutrogena and a philanthropist committed to elevating the profession of teaching). Over dinner we discussed the growing divide between the haves and the have-nots and the racial tensions festering in Los Angeles. "We're sitting on a time bomb," Mr. Riordan remarked.

When Jackie Cotsen found out that Ian and I hadn't yet figured out where we were sleeping that night, she invited us to stay with her. So we spent the night in Bel-Air. I woke up to a gorgeous view of a glistening swimming pool and sun-strewn tennis court.

My trip led me to reflect on the gap between the safe, privileged world of wealthy America and the world in which our corps members were teaching. I wrote to my parents: "The difference is that everything works out in the former world and it doesn't in the latter. Maybe that's just because in the former you can fall a long, long way and still be all right. . . . Anything is possible in the former world and it really isn't in the latter."

The Coup

I had envisioned Teach For America as an organization where all decisions would be made by consensus and where everyone from founder to receptionist would be equally invested in our success. Hierarchy would be unnecessary. People would be assigned different tasks, but there would be no layer between me and anyone else. Every single staff person would make $25,000. All decisions would be made during our communal Monday night meetings.

Although our organizational structure was based on some underlying philosophy, my approach to finding and managing staff was not. I had no idea what to look for in potential staff members. Of course they had to share a deep enthusiasm for our mission, but what else? I lucked into hiring some exceptional people in that first year, but I also picked a few who were less good fits. To make matters worse, I assumed that everyone would simply come through with little or no instruction. When staff members didn't perform at the necessary level, I concluded that they weren't cut out for the job. It never occurred to me that *I* was doing something wrong or that my inexperienced staff members needed more guidance or development.

Another issue was that my personality was not perfectly conducive to the role in which I found myself. I wasn't the type of manager to walk around, rally the troops, and make sure that everyone was feeling good. I would come into the office and spend sixteen straight hours in meetings and on phone calls without even seeing my colleagues.

The biggest problem was that I was as inexperienced as my staff. I had trouble being direct. I floundered when I had issues with staff members' performance. And I now see that I had surprisingly little understanding of the impact my words had on others. I wasn't aware how important it was that my messages foster cooperation and the progress of the organization. Plus, I was so overwhelmed with our daunting financial needs that I had little time to spend on internal issues.

For the first year, when all of our staff members were based in one office and our collective excitement led to a single-minded focus on our mission, we managed to get by despite these problems. But this changed quickly as the organization grew. By the end of year two, we had fifty-five staff members working out of eleven offices. Because of our flat organizational structure, everyone reported to me and so expected me to give them constant encouragement and feedback. I simply couldn't do it; there weren't enough hours in the day. So staff members grew increasingly unhappy. Some even suspected that the reason there were no senior managers was that I wanted to retain full control.

Instead of debating passionately about our mission, we now spent Monday nights squabbling over internal issues: whether we should have a staff dress code, what our compensation structure should be. Few staff members seemed to share my conviction about how quickly we needed to grow or improve. I felt stifled, surrounded by a culture of negativity. Whenever I came up with a new idea about how we should train or support corps members, our worn-down staff greeted it with tears or rolled eyes.

Something needed to be done. Fast. I began working with a small group of staff members to plan a team-based management structure.

But we didn't move rapidly enough. Our problems combusted during our second summer institute in what later became known as the "coup de Kopp." Our entire staff had gathered in Los Angeles for the summer training institute. Unbeknownst to me, almost everyone gathered, too, in underground meetings to discuss how Teach For America should be run. They decided to issue an ultimatum: Either all organizational decisions would be made by vote, or everyone would quit.

On the day the staff would present this plan to me, I had arrived in the office before 6 A.M. (Los Angeles time) to call and fax hundreds of East Coast supporters about our urgent financial needs. Our situation had escalated into a full-blown crisis: We needed $350,000 within two weeks, another $350,000 within the following two weeks, and a total of $1.2 million within two months, by the end of September. That night I stood exhausted in front of a meeting of fifty staff members, who were ready to present me with their ultimatum.

As the staff members fought for their proposal, I struggled with what to do. I envisioned our entire staff leaving the institute, abandoning our seven hundred new corps members. Too tired to think, I let the meeting drag on. Shortly after 10 P.M., Richard Barth raised his hand and asked a leading question: "Wendy, what I think I hear you saying is that you're not going to accept the proposal, and that if people want to leave they can leave. Is that right?" But I couldn't bring myself to be so clear, and I adjourned the meeting, saying I would get back to them the next day.

After a few more hours of debate with myself and discussions with Ian, I determined to do exactly what Richard had tried to suggest. The next morning I issued a memo stating that we would not be making organizational decisions by vote. No one left. But it was hardly a victory. Dissatisfaction was simmering.

A Way Out

During the summer of 1991, when I was deep in the throes of our second summer institute, I received a brochure about an initiative proposed by Chris Whittle, the media entrepreneur who had created Whittle Communications. The brochure announced Whittle's dramatic plans to build a new for-profit school system. Whittle thought big: He intended to open 1,000 schools in short order.

Whittle argued that the very model on which our schools are built doesn't make sense. Look at the grading system, for example, which presumes that half the students are below average; what automaker would assume at the outset that half its cars would fail? Whittle believed we needed a whole new concept of school. He was going to develop this concept through an initiative he called the Edison Project. A play on the Manhattan Project, the name paid tribute to Thomas Edison, who invented the lightbulb rather than improve upon the candle. In the same way, Whittle set out to develop a new type of school rather than simply tinker with the old one.

I was invited to one of dozens of dinners that Whittle held across the country to hear about his idea. After the dinner, I returned to the office on a high. Whittle presented his audacious proposal with conviction. His team shared his enthusiasm.

Whittle invited me to attend a retreat in Knoxville, where his company was headquartered, to discuss the Edison Project at greater length. I jumped at the chance. Expecting to be one of hundreds of enthusiasts, I was shocked to find myself in a quaint country inn with only eight others. For three days, this group debated the idea of the Edison Project.

It turned out that this retreat was Whittle's way of recruiting a start-up team. A few weeks later, I received an offer: I could be a member of the core team of six to ten people, based in Knoxville. I was offered a base salary of $100,000, an equal share in a $5 million core team bonus to be paid when the first schools opened, options that Whittle projected would be worth $5 million ten years after the schools opened, and benefits including first-class travel and a leased car.

This was tempting. Here was an opportunity to join an exciting new adventure. It was also a way to escape Teach For America, which was making me miserable. I imagined myself driving around Knoxville in a red convertible Miata.

But how could I leave Teach For America without making it fall apart? When Whittle later asked me what I thought of his offer, I said I didn't think I could abandon Teach For America. In response, he suggested I meet with Nick Glover, vice chairman of Whittle Communications, who he said would solve all my problems.

The Real Solution

That's exactly what Nick Glover did. He rented a suite in the Waldorf Hotel in New York for a three-day weekend. I was to bring a few of my most trusted staff members. I chose Ian, Daniel, and Richard. We were too overwhelmed with our problems to be fazed by the glamour of the Waldorf and the attention of this important executive. We just dove in and told Nick about the negativity that had pervaded our organization, about the widespread discontent. Nick seemed to understand the situation intuitively.

First, he told us that we needed to get our organization in balance. He pointed out that Ian and I were doing all the fundraising to support the entire program, while sixty or so other staff people focused on recruiting, selecting, training, and supporting corps members. This was not workable. Nick explained that the funding and program sides needed equal energy and that all the other organizational functions would need to support these two sides of the organization equally. I grasped what Nick was saying right away, though it would take me several more years to fully understand the implications of his sage advice.

Next, Nick explained that we would benefit from having a team of leaders with full responsibility for each major area of the organization. In a subtle way, Nick brought us around to the realization that I should not personally do all the strategizing for the organization. Instead, I should find a team of people I believed in and delegate to them. The organization would go further if we put together a group of dedicated individuals and gave them full responsibility, not only to handle projects in their areas but for the strategy and execution necessary to meet their goals.

Nick also showed us how to restructure the relationship between our national and local offices to mitigate the us-versus-them dynamic that had evolved. He suggested we make all the leaders in the national office responsible for our national and local progress in their respective realms. This would ensure that the input and interests of the local offices informed our national policies.

Finally, Nick led us to a viable decisionmaking process. We told him about our Monday night meetings and how despite this laborious system the staff still didn't feel included. Nick explained that this was because twenty-five people could not actually make decisions. The group was too large. "And what about the people who happen to be in the regions?" he asked. It was true; they were simply left out. It would be more effective to establish a core team of people responsible for overarching decisions about organizational structure, expansion, key staffing, and resource allocation.

Nick helped us see where we had gone wrong and what we could do to fix it. He seemed to understand entrepreneurs, to have an implicit respect for them, and to truly enjoy helping them hurdle the obstacles that came between them and their visions.

Following Nick's advice, I asked Daniel to be the vice president of program and Ian to be the vice president of development. Richard wanted to remain our executive director in charge of the New York local office. Jim Filoso, our Georgia executive director, came to the national office to handle our staffing and human resources issues. The five of us formed the management team.

Two weekends later we flew all of our managers to Atlanta for a conference where Nick Glover presented our new management structure. After the conference I went on a five-day whirlwind tour of all eleven of our offices, personally explaining our new setup to staff members.

It worked. Within weeks Teach For America felt like a different place. As I entrusted more of the organization to others, we began accomplishing more and I became less overwhelmed. And people seemed relieved to know that there was a team of people leading us forward.

Nick Glover had succeeded perfectly in doing what Chris Whittle had asked him to do: He helped me get Teach For America to a manageable point so that I could turn it over to someone else. Perhaps he succeeded too perfectly. As I became happier in my own organization, I also began to think that I could make us grow into the effective movement I wanted us to be.

Daniel, Ian, Richard, and I convened at the bustling Café Lalo in the West Eighties to discuss my future. Should I join Edison, or should I stay with Teach For America? Over the next two hours, we fleshed out an inspiring vision of Teach For America's future. I decided to stay.

I had in my hands a first-class ticket to Knoxville for the following Monday to join the seven other members of Whittle's core team. I agonized. I felt terribly guilty rejecting Whittle's offer, especially when he had helped me revive Teach For America. Finally, I sent him a fax. It was over. I was staying.

Teach For America's organizational difficulties had taken their toll. We recruited and trained 700 new corps members in our second year and only 550 in our third. But we had refined our approach to selecting and training corps members. We had beefed up our systems for providing them with ongoing support. We had raised the funding we needed to cover our costs. And Nick Glover had restored my sense of possibility. With the lessons he taught us, I figured we could accomplish anything.

Chapter 4

New Ideas

During my first summer after graduation, in my tour of the country to sell Teach For America, I had talked extensively with Michael Brown, the cofounder of City-Year. Michael told me that the most important thing to remember was to "just say no." He explained that there would be many people along the way— funders, staff members, educators—who would want Teach For America to pursue other missions. The most important thing I could do, he said, was to remember my mission and stick to it.

I remembered this advice when it came to considering the ideas of others. It was my own imagination that got me in trouble. It wasn't as if Teach For America offered no remaining programmatic challenges to keep me busy. In fact, I was working closely with our staff to discover how we could help corps members become more effective. How could we refine our selection model to ensure that all of our corps members would have what it took to excel at the intensely challenging job of teaching? How could our institute provide corps members with the tools not only to survive as teachers but to thrive? What exactly should our support directors be doing to provide corps members with the best possible professional development? What else should we be doing to build a sense of esprit de corps? What more could we do, at each stage of our programmatic continuum, to ensure that corps members would approach their students and communities with openness and sensitivity? I was immersed in these challenges, and they should have been more than enough to keep me intellectually engaged.

But a mere year into Teach For America I began thinking about what else had to be done to improve education. Teach For America was providing about 500 new teachers each year; meanwhile, school systems were hiring about 200,000 new teachers each year. Even if Teach For America tripled or quadrupled in size, we would still provide only a small fraction of the new teachers hired. It struck me that we should help school systems do what we did: bring outstanding people into the teaching profession. What we were doing wasn't rocket science. We were recruiting terrific people through aggressive outreach and smart messages, selecting those who demonstrated exemplary personal characteristics, and training and supporting them. School districts could do the same.

But they didn't. District officials relied on schools of education to find teachers for them, and they generally resigned themselves to picking only from the annual pool of education majors who took the initiative to apply for jobs. This would be fine, except that schools of education weren't supplying enough bright, diverse people to meet districts' needs. In some cases districts had created "alternate route" programs to enable people without teaching certificates to teach, but these programs generally lacked the vigorous recruitment strategies needed to attract truly outstanding candidates.

I thought districts should go after the most talented education majors and also recruit as far beyond education schools as necessary to find enough people who met their standards. I was imagining developing within school districts a whole new mindset—the belief that public schools could and should compete with other sectors for talented people—as well as the outreach and marketing capacity to act on that belief.

Not only did districts in urban and rural areas rarely launch aggressive recruitment campaigns, but most also lacked rigorous processes for screening applicants. I knew firsthand about the New York City selection process because I went through it myself. Our staff had applied for temporary licenses so that we could substitute teach and thus better understand what our corps members and their students were going through every day. At that time the process—which was the same for substitute teachers as it was for other new teachers—left much to be desired. First, the roomful of applicants was asked to write a one-page essay. The proctor reassured us that form, not content, was what counted; if we dotted our i's and crossed our t's we should be okay. Then I went through an "interview." After five minutes, during which time I clearly didn't provide the portly, gray-haired, and very kind gentleman who interviewed me with the answer he was looking for, he said, "Oh, you're all right," chuckled, and let me go.

We also knew that districts weren't investing a great deal in the development of their new teachers. Our corps members were lucky if they got a general orientation and a visit from their school principal each year. They weren't provided with intensive orientations about the mission of their schools and districts. And they didn't receive nearly enough help in honing the skills they would need to be effective teachers.

This needed to change if our school districts were to become more successful. Every good organization in every other sector spends tremendous amounts of energy and resources on recruiting, selecting, training, and developing their staff and leadership. Organizations make this investment because they know that the surest way to meet their goals is to have great people at every level. (My own experience in addressing the organizational difficulties at Teach For America reinforced my conviction on this score.) I became convinced that the superintendents who made this issue a top priority could revolutionize their school systems within just a few years. The teachers they hired would almost immediately raise student achievement rates, and some of them could be molded into school principals within three to five years.

Having seen all this up close, I thought, "Why not launch an organization that would help school systems develop the means to effectively recruit, select, train, and support new teachers?" Along with Richard, Ian, and others, I dreamed up an organization dubbed TEACH! that would contract with school systems to do just this. It wasn't long before I was quite taken with this plan. I couldn't stop myself from growing more and more excited about it.

At the same time, I began thinking that even with TEACH! we could not solve all the problems facing today's disadvantaged students. As long as teachers were working within the limits of today's schools, they could not ensure their students would fulfill their true potential. As Chris Whittle had said, we needed a new concept of school. Our management team dreamed up another idea: We would run summer programs for students to free ourselves from the regulations governing schools. The summer programs would allow us to think outside the box about what schools should really be like. Once our summer programs began attaining results, parents would insist the programs become year-round. Ultimately, we imagined, we could run hundreds of innovative schools all over the country. We would call this effort The Learning Project.

Chapter 5

The Dark Years

As we dreamed up new ideas, our effort to grow and sustain Teach For America ran up against a roadblock. In the for-profit world there is one set of venture capital firms to provide start-up support and another group of firms to provide "mezzanine" capital to help start-ups make the transition to a more advanced stage. While I had been able to secure start-up support from national corporations and foundations, the mezzanine structure does not exist in the nonprofit world. So as of our fourth year, when we would begin to lose many of the grants we had received, we had no alternative national funding source to turn to. This didn't mean we would never again receive funding from these sources; they would still be open to funding proposals for special projects that were in line with their priorities. But they didn't want to fund our core mission.

At the same time that some foundations decided they had to move on to new programs, others told us they were concerned about the effectiveness of the training and support we were providing corps members. Despite all that we had invested in developing an effective professional development program, there was more to be done. We knew this, which is why we kept hiring more support directors and increasing the budget. But we also felt this issue was indicative of a larger problem in the way districts were bringing new teachers into the profession. Other new teachers didn't receive effective training and support either.

Another thing I learned from people in the philanthropic community was that they were generally more interested in "systemic" initiatives. "What is your plan to have a systemic influence?" they would ask. At first I wasn't completely clear what "systemic" meant, but ultimately I gathered it referred to programs that would effect fundamental, far-reaching, long-term change. There wasn't yet evidence that our corps members would be lifelong education advocates, and potential funders didn't see my vision that Teach For America was a critical part of a long-term approach to education reform because it provided its future leadership.

TEACH! seemed to be the answer not only to the problems of teacher quality but also to these funders' questions. It was a new program. It would create a high-quality professional development program that would work not only for Teach For America corps members but for other new teachers. It was certainly systemic.

So our management team developed a plan: We would set up local organizations to recruit, select, train, and support teachers for school districts; the districts would pay for our services, thus ensuring they were truly invested in our approach and that the change was in fact systemic. We envisioned a major national initiative with twenty-five contracts across the country within two years. Ultimately, TEACH! would support itself on revenue from these contracts; we just needed a few years of start-up funding.

We planned to put the responsibility for perfecting Teach For America's teacher training and support model on the staff of TEACH!, the organization that would ultimately apply the model more broadly. This way, Teach For America could focus on its core mission—being a service corps that recruited corps members and rallied them together through local gatherings, newsletters, and the like—and TEACH! could set out on its mission to revolutionize the way new teachers are brought into the profession. By training and supporting Teach For America corps members, TEACH! would be able to test and demonstrate to districts and states an effective professional development program. To get started, we would transfer some of Teach For America's existing staff over to TEACH! in order to give TEACH! the infrastructure to run the training and support program and to market its services to districts across the country. Thus, our plan decreased Teach For America's costs while building an even stronger program for the ongoing training of Teach For America corps members.

Just as I had done with Teach For America a few years before, I launched TEACH! before securing the financial commitments to fund its activities. I was sure that just as foundations and corporations had invested millions of dollars into Teach For America, they would invest millions in this new initiative, which was exactly what they seemed to be looking for. We also began The Learning Project, in an effort to develop a better model for schools. It required only a small team with modest expenses, so I decided to fund it out of our general operating budget.

I appointed Dan Porter, a Princeton grad who had taught for a year in Brooklyn before joining our staff during our first year, to be the president of Teach For America. Richard became the president of TEACH! Daniel became the president of The Learning Project. I managed the three of them as the president of TFA, Inc., our holding organization. I thought this was a great plan. This new structure would expand our impact, and it would solve our funding problems. The only catch: Our funders didn't see it that way.

The Tide Turns

In his book *The New New Thing,* Michael Lewis captured the essence of the Internet era through the story of Jim Clark, one of its most exalted entrepreneurs. The mastermind behind Netscape and Healtheon, Clark spent his time coming up with "the new new thing"—the latest idea that would be even bigger and better than the last one. He was an ideas machine. In that era, venture capitalists fell all over each other to get the chance to fund the new new proposal from entrepreneurs like Clark whose previous ventures worked, even if the new new proposal seemed risky or unlikely. The bolder the better. Experimentation was good. Youth was an asset. In the education arena in 1993, this was not how things worked.

By this time my access to corporate CEOs or foundation heads had become more limited than before; now that their organizations had developed more concrete funding guidelines for education, many chief executives were hesitant to interfere with their staff's processes. So I was working with program officers in large philanthropic foundations such as the Carnegie Corporation, the Lilly Endowment, and the Kellogg Foundation, as well as executives who ran the foundations or giving departments within large corporations.

With many potential funders, I encountered skepticism. New prospects didn't know what to make of me. The head of one major foundation, who sat next to me at an education conference, once asked me, "Now, who's *behind* this? Who's in *charge?*" When I explained that I was, he said, "No, no. I mean, who's the *driving* force? Who's the chairman of the board?"

Our past supporters were confused. They didn't understand the relationship between Teach For America and TEACH! They thought we were taking on too much. Neither did they see why we needed a whole organization to help districts recruit and train teachers; wouldn't it be easier simply to lobby for the changes to take place? And how could we hope to revolutionize teacher quality without working with schools of education? After all, it was schools of education that provided the vast majority of the nation's teachers.

As I saw it, these people were missing the point. It wasn't that I thought schools of education weren't important. I just couldn't understand how we expected school systems to work if they didn't invest in recruiting and developing their own staffs. And I also figured that our strategy would encourage schools of education to improve; if they didn't, school systems wouldn't hire their graduates. But I was fighting a losing battle. At one foundation the program officer advised me, out of the goodness of her heart, to focus my energy elsewhere: "Wendy, this foundation funds the establishment to reform the establishment."

Still, we made some progress in selling TEACH! Adele Simmons, president of the MacArthur Foundation, thought the idea was so strong that she agreed to host and attend a meeting of national foundation officers to discuss it. Thanks to program officer Rick Love, the Knight Foundation committed $1 million over two years. The Walton Foundation and the Luce Foundation made significant pledges as well. All in all, we raised about $3 million over two years. But that wasn't enough. TFA, Inc. couldn't scare up the funding we needed for our fourth fiscal year. We raised $7.8 million—$600,000 short of expenditures.

Although we were having trouble securing the funding, TEACH! was beginning to come together. We had laid important groundwork, forming a board of advisers that included such educational heavyweights as Al Shanker, the revered president of the American Federation of Teachers; David Hornbeck, who at the time represented the Business Roundtable in its calls for systemic change at the state level; John Anderson, who would go on to lead the heavily funded New American Schools Development Corporation; and Kati Haycock, a highly respected advocate for equity in education.

Richard had hired Joe Fernandez, the recently retired chancellor of New York City's public schools, to arrange meetings with school system superintendents. Richard attended about twenty-five of these meetings. Most of the superintendents were extremely receptive; they embraced the idea that good, smart hires were the key to their success. Now the challenge was to get them to make the necessary investments and sign on the dotted line.

To buttress its professional development model, TEACH! hired enough staff to enable a ratio of one support director for every twenty-five corps members. And based on this model, TEACH! gained approval to run alternate routes to teacher certification in rural North Carolina, Baltimore, Oakland, and Compton, California. This was the first step to running state-approved programs for school districts.

Even though the funding community hadn't donated the full amount we had requested, I didn't contemplate giving up on TEACH! now. Too many people had already invested in it; I didn't want to let down the funders or the staff. And I was convinced that TEACH!

would have a powerful impact on the way new teachers were brought into the profession. I decided to progress by lowering the TEACH! budget. This meant that Teach For America would need to cover the corps members' professional development costs. If TEACH! wasn't the solution, there had to be another.

Staying Afloat

We owed $600,000 to UCLA, which had hosted our 1993 summer institute. The only way to stay afloat was to delay paying that bill. The debt hung over my head, but not nearly as much as knowing we had to meet a $200,000 payroll every two weeks. I was terrified that one day we wouldn't be able to pay our already financially strapped staff members. At this time all of us were making less than $50,000, and most were making closer to $25,000. (Nick Glover had counseled us out of our initially purely egalitarian compensation structure.) If we missed a payroll, people wouldn't be able to pay their rent or have money for meals. I couldn't let this happen. Fear that it might kept me going.

Every other week we would come dangerously close to falling short of the $200,000 we needed. A knot of tension formed and grew in my chest. I slept little and worked as hard as I had ever worked in my life. I tried to maximize every minute of every workday to talk with potential funders.

Midway into October 1993, one month into our fifth fiscal year, I called our most loyal funders once again and explained the dire situation we were in: We would be completely out of money by the following week, and I had no prospects. Several of the people I called talked with each other and got back to me with their conclusions: (1)

We needed to hire a professional fundraiser; (2) we needed a three-year business plan; and (3) we needed to reach Michael Milken (who had led the revolution in junk bond financing before being barred from working in the securities industry), who they had heard would be spending millions on improving education.

I knew that a development professional and a three-year business plan would not enable me to meet payroll the following week. So I focused on the Michael Milken idea, which seemed like a pragmatic approach given the immediacy of our problem. I happened to be in Los Angeles at the time, and I heard that Mr. Milken was teaching a class at the UCLA business school. Whatever it took, I was going to meet him.

I snuck past the security guards at the entrance to Milken's class—they must have thought I was a student—and slid into an empty seat at the back of the small room. Milken entered, exuding energy and intensity. I was aware of his controversial past, but he certainly came across as a passionate visionary concerned about making the world a better place. He devoted a solid portion of the class to stressing the point that businesses committed to communities are stronger businesses. At the end of a dynamic three-hour show, I walked up to him and introduced myself. He knew who I was and said he wanted to talk to me! We were both heading to the East Coast the following day. He offered to take me back in his private plane. Needless to say, this was not my usual mode of transportation. I accepted the offer.

Half terrified—how was I going to make conversation with this man all the way from Los Angeles to New York?—and half ecstatic—this simply *had* to be my answer—I showed up at the airport and waited to board the airplane. Mr. Milken's wife, his son, his sister and her husband, and his brother's two sons were all waiting to fly back with him as well. They warned me that Mr. Milken would be late; he was always late. When he finally arrived, we all boarded a little plane, decked out with a luxurious interior.

I talked to Michael Milken, with no distractions, for three and a half hours. He told me how impressed he was with Teach For America, how interesting it was that I had taken this on and had seen so much of the world in a mere four years. He gave me a one-hour course on the history of "change agents"—people who try to change the course of history. (His version was that they are all killed.) We spent another hour comparing education reform philosophies. Then I asked him for a million dollars.

I tried and tried to get him to make a commitment before the plane landed. One million dollars would be the difference between life and death for Teach For America, I told him. It was a small amount to him, but it would make a huge difference to us. I said this over and over. He was extremely encouraging. He said he would help me, but he couldn't commit until he talked it over with a few people. He promised to call me on Monday. We landed in Philadelphia, and his limo dropped me off at the train station. I took the 1:30 A.M. train home to New York. I was on an incredible high, certain that this multimillionaire would come through for me. What was $1 million to him?

What I didn't realize was that Mr. Milken would rely on the education program officer in his foundation for advice. Unfortunately, this gentleman didn't like Teach For America; I already knew this, having debated the issue with him for hours on several occasions. Despite repeated calls and faxes, I never talked to Michael Milken again.

But somehow, even without his help, we pulled together enough money for payroll. By holding off on paying bills and securing the cash for every single national and regional funding commitment as soon as they were made, we survived another two weeks. And then another two weeks. And then another.

But our perilous financial situation only further weakened our credibility in the funding community. In December 1993 we brought some of our major funders together in an effort to inspire their confidence in our plan. In a brief letter they advised us to retain an experienced business manager or chief operating officer, develop a long-term business plan with the help of an outside management organization, and retain an experienced development director to coordinate national and local fundraising efforts. They also suggested that we start TEACH! as a pilot program rather than as the major national initiative we had planned.

I feared that no one would step in as chief operating officer at this juncture. Things were too overwhelming and relied too much on my knowledge of what we were doing. And we had already developed a long-term plan. Our corporate and foundation supporters had warned Ian and me as early as our second year that we would have to figure out how to sustain ourselves long term without their grants. In search of a dependable stream of money, we went to Washington, D.C., to explore the possibility of securing federal funding. Not convinced that federal support would be forthcoming, we tried to figure out ways to form a mutually beneficial, revenue-generating relationship with an educational supply company. Or, we thought, perhaps TEACH! would one day generate funds for our program.

We considered and dismissed other possibilities. We did not want to ask corps members to pay us. One of our principles was that we had to recruit teachers as aggressively into Teach For America as they were being recruited into investment banks; how could we ask them to pay? Among other things, that would ruin our effort to recruit college seniors of all socioeconomic backgrounds.

Nor did we think the solution was to charge school districts for our services. Some of our districts might agree to pay. But others seemed so plagued by politics or a lack of resources that it would be impossible to get such a proposal through their school boards. We did not think we had the leverage to overcome these challenges everywhere, and we felt strongly that our ability to fulfill our mission required that we continue to work with districts irrespective of their willingness or ability to pay.

Finally, we had zeroed in on a promising strategy: building significant bases of private philanthropic support in the local areas where we placed corps members. This seemed to make sense. Local donors would support our mission in the communities where our immediate impact was felt most closely. We were moving forward in building our local capacity to raise funds, but Ian and I were so pressed to meet payroll that immediate needs took priority. Moreover, it took time to build regional boards and relationships with regional funders. We needed some interim solutions.

I wasn't opposed to the idea of hiring a professional fundraiser; I just hadn't found the right person. The development professionals I contacted would not offer us access to their thick Rolodexes. Instead, these professionals would simply advise us on how we could best leverage the relationships we already had and on how to put together an internal infrastructure to develop additional relationships over time. But I had already worn out our welcome with our existing contacts, and we didn't have time to build our long-term development capacity. We needed money fast.

Our situation was unique, and few professionals could understand how we had even made it this far. Back then, we were one of very few national K–12 education organizations, and the others were headed by influential leaders. In fact, in 1993 Teach For America was ranked third in the *Chronicle of Philanthropy*'s "top ten recipients of foundation grants" in the area of elementary and secondary education. We were listed right behind the Fund for New York City Public Education, a consortium of leaders in New York's business, philanthropic, and education communities, and the National Board for Professional Teaching Standards, whose sixty-three-member board included not only the most highly recognizable and respected educators in the country but governors and corporate leaders.

In the larger scheme of things, we really didn't need that much money. But funders saw that we had no money and in turn told us they were too concerned about our viability to give us any. One foundation wouldn't even look at our proposal because we had run a deficit the year before. Of course this created a self-fulfilling prophecy.

Why I Persisted

With each month things only became worse. By now all my time went into finding the $200,000 we needed to make payroll every two weeks.

It was a bizarre situation. Here I was, waking up each day to the fear that we might not raise the funding we needed, while one thousand Teach For America corps members went about their teaching. Day in and day out, they were working in one of the thirteen geographic regions where we had placed them. They were struggling to help kids fulfill their potential everywhere from the Rio Grande Valley in Texas to

Oakland, California, to Baltimore City. They were working their hearts out, acting out the mission of Teach For America, generally oblivious that Teach For America was about to go under.

It surely would have helped me guide our program and organization if I had gotten out into our schools more. But I couldn't justify spending my time visiting classrooms when I could be calling funders instead. So I went on blind faith that Teach For America was working as I hoped. And as our corps members plugged away, I forced myself to persist with each prospect even when all indications were that there was no hope. This provided for some humorous instances.

In one case I had been rejected four years in a row by a particular foundation. I kept sending proposals. Every three months or so, I would brace myself, call the program officer, and ask her how things looked. Whenever she would agree to get together, I would try again to sell her on the missions of Teach For America and TEACH! At one particularly stressful juncture, we scheduled yet another meeting. Hoping this would be the one, I geared up for it. The program officer appeared with materials for another organization, Recruiting New Teachers. She proceeded to take notes about everything I said in tiny print, in pencil, down the margins of a letter from this other organization. I couldn't imagine what she was thinking, but she seemed to be following our conversation, so I kept on. About fifty minutes into the meeting, she evidently realized her mistake. Without any hesitation at all, as I continued talking, she spent fifteen minutes vigorously erasing the entire page of notes. I couldn't decide whether to laugh or cry.

In a subsequent phone call, this program officer confided in me. She was burdened with an incredible workload. "Wendy, can't you and Recruiting New Teachers and some of these other groups get together and do a joint proposal?" she asked. "It is just so difficult to decide between everything." I guess I ultimately wore her down, because one day a year later I got a call saying the foundation had approved a grant of $150,000 over two years.

There were also instances when our funders acted like guardian angels. One of the most amazing shows of support came in the spring of 1994 from Lee Walcott, who directed the education program at the Ahmanson Foundation. I had asked Mr. Walcott to consider renewing our $250,000 grant earlier than usual. He agreed. The day our grant was up for board approval I called again, this time to ask whether he might be able to wire the funds directly into our account if the grant were approved. The grant would enable us to make payroll the next day. Without mentioning the precariousness of this plan, he agreed to see what he could do. Later I discovered he sold his board on the idea that even though Ahmanson was decreasing the size of many of its grants, it should give Teach For America even more than we had asked for because of the tough financial spot we were in. The next day Mr. Walcott called to say that he was wiring $350,000 into our account. Without that grant, Teach For America probably wouldn't have survived those difficult months.

Help from Washington

While we lurched from payroll to payroll, I was trying to secure a federal grant that would alleviate our problems. It seemed logical to me that we would be able to get some kind of appropriation through the Elementary and Secondary Education Act, whose purpose was to strengthen K–12 education in low-income areas. Why wouldn't the federal government fund the national teacher corps? It saw fit to invest

$194 million a year in the Peace Corps ($30,000 per corps member). We were seeking only a few million dollars; a mere $4,000 per corps member would have made up half of our total budget.

My argument didn't seem to strike a chord with the government officials I met. Instead, they suggested we try to get in on newly elected President Clinton's plans for launching a domestic service corps. So I began working with the administration to shape the legislation in a way that would make it possible for organizations like us to get funding. Clinton had originally envisioned a corps that would enable talented individuals to serve as lawyers, police officers, and teachers in low-income areas, but the draft legislation was geared toward a youth corps that would enlist young people, both with and without college degrees, to perform service activities such as tutoring and environmental cleanup. In this model, corps members would receive a low stipend as well as a $5,000 "education award" that could be spent toward past and future educational expenses.

I made the case for including a professional corps model where highly qualified college graduates could meet pressing needs in low-income areas at regular salaries. I felt our model could be applied, with some modifications, to fields like medicine, law enforcement, pre-school education, even architecture. Weren't professional corps a necessary part of national service? They would make service attractive to some potential recruits who might not consider joining a youth corps, and they would show young people that they could have full careers in public service. Moreover, I figured that professional corps would have the same kind of short-term and long-term impact in other sectors that Teach For America would in education.

In 1994 the legislation was passed. It created the Corporation for National Service, a public-private agency that would fund nonprofit organizations to operate AmeriCorps programs. The legislation authorized the Corporation to include professional corps.

A total of $40 million was to be distributed among various national organizations running service corps. (Millions more had been appropriated for local organizations running local corps.) Now we just needed to convince the Corporation to give Teach For America some of that money. We wrote a solid application, following the guidance we had received not to apply for more than $2 million.

Although the officials at the Corporation told us our written application was strong, they were concerned about our financial stability. They were worried that even with an operating grant of $2 million, we would not be able to meet our operating budget of $8 million. It occurred to me that if they were really concerned about our financial stability, they could have offered us, say, $3 million, which would be $3,000 per corps member. But I also understood they were reserving the vast majority of funds for new programs rather than preexisting ones.

I spent hours on the phone and in meetings trying to convince top officials of the Corporation for National Service to make the grant. Then its chief financial officer decided to settle the matter once and for all by sending up a financial director on loan from the Department of Agriculture. I was absolutely terrified. This man was going to spend two days with us and then make a recommendation about whether we were worthy of AmeriCorps's $2 million. It seemed that every person we encountered was critical of our situation. Why would this man be any different?

I was shocked, therefore, to meet a friendly Washingtonian with no preconceptions, a relaxed, bearish guy in his fifties who appeared on our doorstep in khaki pants and a short-sleeved oxford. He smiled when he met us. He seemed to think this was fun. For two hours, he sat in our offices; listened to us describe our financial history, challenges, and progress; and read over all sorts of papers he had requested that documented our revenues, expenses, and cash-flow situation. After those two hours, he leaned back, announced that he was impressed, and told us that we were going to be all right. He was going to show us how to present ourselves in a way that would be satisfactory to the executives at the Corporation for National Service. I was flabbergasted. I simply couldn't believe it. He was going to help us!

With his help we were able to convince the Corporation for National Service that with their grant, we would be able to survive financially. They came through with a grant of $2 million and transferred the funds earlier than their regular grant schedule in order to accommodate our timeline. (Unlike most AmeriCorps members, Teach For America corps members begin their commitment with our summer training institute rather than in the fall; this fact would ultimately create great consternation in our relationship with AmeriCorps.)

This time Teach For America owed its evasion of financial ruin to this one individual, who came into our lives for a mere two days and was willing to overlook that our CFO was not a CPA and that we were a bunch of kids a few years out of college. I tried to contact him several times after he left our offices to thank him for his help, but he never returned my call, and I learned soon thereafter that he had left the Department of Agriculture.

Rallying to Prepare the Corps

The commitment from the Corporation for National Service came just in time to pay the bill for our 1994 summer institute. Officials at the University of Houston allowed us to sign a contract and let our staff set up shop just a few days before corps members would arrive on campus.

That summer institute would be another rocky one. A few months earlier we had come up with the idea that we could save lots of money—and improve the program—by moving the institute out of Los Angeles. We had initially chosen Los Angeles because it was the only city that could accommodate each of our 500 corps members in a different classroom for student teaching. But the student teaching was far from ideal. There were significant inconsistencies among the 500 master teachers. Moreover, there were limitations on what corps members could experience in any classroom where the tone and systems were established by a veteran teacher.

We might have lived with these problems if our financial situation had allowed it. But the institute was costing us $2 million a year in Los Angeles, and we figured that we could dramatically decrease costs if we moved to a cheaper area of the country, ran our own summer school for students, and arranged for a partnering school district to cover some of our expenses in exchange. We began contacting dozens of school districts all across the country. In March 1994 I decided to move the institute to Houston, Texas, where the Houston Independent School District had agreed to absorb some of our costs.

Understandably, many of our staff were unhappy about the move. How, in a mere three months, were we going to design a whole new institute, including a summer school program for students, and then train the faculty to run it? My solution was to ask our most talented programmatic mind, Daniel Oscar, to take over.

Daniel had spent his previous few months working with a three-person team to develop plans for summer school programs for the following summer. Now The Learning Project had a more urgent responsibility, and Daniel and his team dove into their tall task with gusto. In three months they ironed out the details with Houston's school district, convinced ten principals to turn their schools over to us, recruited thousands of students, recruited and trained a faculty, created a curriculum, and pulled together the resources to implement it.

We packed our 500 corps members into one seventeen-story dorm, complete with two very slow elevators, on the campus of the University of Houston. We took over the lounges on each floor to set up makeshift computer rooms and teacher resource rooms. At around 6 A.M. each day, corps members would line up outside, in professional dress, to board yellow school buses that waited to take them to the schools where they would work in teams of three or four to teach classes and go through afternoon professional development sessions with our faculty of Teach For America alumni. In the evenings they were back on campus in workshops, lesson-planning meetings, and never-ending lines for the two copy machines.

The good news was that the institute happened and that it cost us $1 million less than it had the previous year. Moreover, this new training model ultimately proved to be far superior to what we could have achieved by refining the program in Los Angeles. This experience taught me that it's not always a bad thing to have limited resources. They can inspire creative thinking and force through difficult decisions.

The bad news was that corps members again had good cause to be frustrated at our disorganization. Because we had had too little time to prepare for a brand new training approach in a brand new place, systems were lacking. There weren't enough students for the summer schools, our faculty didn't fully understand the new model, and the cafeteria wasn't prepared for so many vegetarians.

I was scheduled to make a speech to the corps midway through the institute. Although virtually all of our corps members were working hard and staying focused on their training, tensions were high. This was not the time for me to gather the corps and make a big speech. After addressing the history and future of Teach For America, I opened the floor to questions. In short order things got out of hand. Some corps members stood on chairs and yelled at me; a deaf corps member cursed at me through her interpreter; another corps member admonished me for never having taught. That night has gone down in history as "the night of a thousand suggestions." Some alumni came to my defense. One stood up on a chair and gave an impassioned speech about the fact that we were all in this together: "Corps is staff and staff is corps," she pleaded, to no avail.

I remained calm throughout this ordeal. I realized that the corps members were somewhat justified in their criticisms, but I also knew that we had done just about everything in our power to hold things together and make the institute possible at all. Also, I had lived through similar sessions during our first and second institutes, and by now I had the perspective to realize that this, too, would pass. Like the others before them, this corps would begin teaching and quickly realize that there were greater challenges than being cooped up at the summer institute.

The Last Straw

I needed a break. At the end of that exhausting summer, I went to the Jersey shore for a week with Richard Barth, whom I had started dating a few months earlier. Richard and I spent our days sleeping on the beach and trying to relax. But all was not well. During that week my assistant faxed me an article that had just appeared in the September 1994 issue of *Phi Delta Kappan,* the journal of the academic education community. Linda Darling-Hammond, then a professor at Columbia's Teachers College, chose this time to publish a lengthy article about Teach For America entitled "Who Will Speak for the Children?"

"In this article," Darling-Hammond wrote, "I examine TFA's track record, training, assessments, and operations in terms of their capacity to ensure that TFA-trained candidates are adequately prepared to meet the needs of their students. On each of these dimensions, TFA's shortcomings are serious, and they ultimately hurt many schools and the children in them." For fourteen pages, the article supported Darling-Hammond's conclusion with analyses of the media coverage about Teach For America and quotes from disgruntled corps members, school administrators, and former staff.

I didn't even recognize the organization she was describing. We had huge challenges, but not in the ways she was portraying them. Darling-Hammond repeated her harsh assessment over and over: "The costs of TFA to city schools and children are clearly large in human terms," she stated at one point. At another point she wrote that Teach For America "is especially disturbing to those who are concerned about the well-being of children in the poor rural and urban districts that TFA has targeted."

Darling-Hammond portrayed Teach For America as an organization that worked for its own interest against the interests of helpless communities: "In many places, parents, other teachers, and district administrators are angry about the chaos TFA recruits have left behind when they couldn't handle the job. These feelings run deep in minority communities, where good intentions that fail to produce good teaching for African American and Latino children look like a thin veil for arrogance, condescension, and continuing neglect."

This article was like a punch in the chest. I read it more as a personal attack than an academic analysis of our efforts. I felt it was based on a misunderstanding of our intentions. We were trying to help. In fact, the school districts and school principals we served appreciated our help. Schools of education had not met their needs, and we were filling the gap.

I knew I would have to respond to the allegations contained in the article. So while still on vacation I began to dissect Darling-Hammond's argument and to draft a response for circulation among our supporters. In doing so, I grew all the more amazed that Darling-Hammond's article could pass the research standards of the *Phi Delta Kappan*. In one instance Darling-Hammond used as evidence an article in *Newsday*: "Of the several recruits the article covered," wrote Darling-Hammond, "a number of them were in 'extreme doubt' and three quit before the first week of school was over, leaving their students with no teachers at all and their schools scrambling to find substitutes." When I went back and looked at the *Newsday* article, I discovered that it had been written a week after Teach For America placed its first corps members in September 1990. It followed one Teach For America corps member through his first week and noted that five others were teaching in his school. The original article had quoted their principal, Katherine Solomon: "I'm so pleased with these little ones, with their enthusiasm, their commitment. . . . They want to do so much that it shows all over them. I have to get them out of the school at the end of the day—they won't leave." The article stated that three of the 177 corps members who had been placed in New York had not finished their first week.

At another point, Darling-Hammond quoted the deputy chancellor of the New York City school system, Beverly Hall, recalling that "the candidates were so poorly prepared that a number had to be let go—but not before they had undermined the education of the children they were assigned to teach." How could this be? Dr. Hall had been a strong supporter of Teach For America. When we called to ask if she had made this statement, she told me that she had not. (She later became the superintendent of the Newark Unified School District and then of the Atlanta Public Schools, and in both positions she brought Teach For America into her district.)

Darling-Hammond also quoted one principal as stating that the corps members were ineffective and "not really dedicated." Yet in the spring before the article was published, Teach For America had conducted and disseminated a survey of the principals who hired corps members. We received responses from 233 principals, representing schools in which 642 corps members were teaching. More than 95 percent of the principals reported that corps members were at least as good as, if not better than, their other beginning teachers; 67 percent said that Teach For America corps members were better than their other new teachers. And more than 60 percent rated them as better than their *overall teaching faculty.*

I called a number of our supporters in the education community to ask how we should respond publicly. They advised me to lie low. They didn't think we had the credibility to win an all-out war. And no one volunteered to come to our defense. So I wrote a relatively subdued letter to the editor correcting the article's most outrageous claims in a factual tone. Darling-Hammond replied with a harsh letter of her own, four times as long as mine, which was printed in the same issue.

I weighed the pros and cons of meeting Darling-Hammond directly to talk out the issues she raised. Having heard of her opposition to our effort before the article was published, we had invited her to meet with members of our staff and to review our evaluations. She already had as much evidence as I would be able to provide in a meeting. Besides, in the article she also described an earlier meeting between us so inaccurately that I assumed that future meetings would simply provide more fodder for her diatribes.

I had assumed that the article was so over the top that no one would take it seriously. I was wrong. Funders called for reassurances and answers to the questions that Darling-Hammond had raised. For years afterward, every article about us in the national media would quote Linda Darling-Hammond. When I distributed an analysis of the evidence presented in the article, readers were simply confused about whom and what to believe.

But we were in no position to defend Teach For America. I was preoccupied with our mounting organizational woes. As our fiscal year drew to a close in September, revenues once again came in $600,000 lower than expenses. We had raised $8.5 million and spent $9.1 million. This made our cumulative deficit $1.2 million. We stayed afloat by again delaying the $600,000 UCLA bill, securing a loan of about $450,000 from some of our initial funders, and holding off many other vendors to whom we owed money.

As stressful as our financial situation was, internal staff problems grew to become at least as debilitating. The constant pressure and last-minute crises generated by our lack of money were demoralizing. Moreover, with so many layers and such overwhelmed leadership, the culture of the organization had deteriorated. Staff members of TEACH! and Teach For America were doing things to undermine each other. I got the impression some people were more interested in looking good than doing what was right for the organization. I even discovered a few glaring examples of dishonesty. Once I found out that Teach For America's funding plan—which was the basis of our cash-flow projections—was filled with fake prospects. Our organization reminded me of *Lord of the Flies*. All these people were running around with no common goals, no unifying values.

Chapter 6

Big Decisions

One day on my way home from the airport, I pulled out my laptop and began writing down how I believed everyone at Teach For America should operate. I had learned, upon checking my messages when the plane landed, of yet another incident that was evidence of our corroding culture. It sent me over the edge. I still remember sitting in the back of a cab typing furiously into my computer.

First I wrote "good writing, thinking, and speaking." I felt that everyone on our staff should be equally committed to producing well-written documents and ensuring that our strategies and approaches were well conceived.

"Responsibility" came next. I wanted everyone to feel accountable for the success of the larger organization, to operate with a sense of loyalty to the whole. I wanted to see people following through on their commitments and taking the initiative to improve things rather than sitting back and complaining.

Then I wrote "constant learning." It seemed the biggest problem we faced was that people saw critical feedback as a sign that they weren't successful, which led them to try to hide what they were doing from their managers. This meant that it was extraordinarily difficult to ensure quality or develop people's skills. The year before, I had read a book called *Surpassing Ourselves,* written by two cognitive psychologists who had studied the characteristics that distinguished "experts" from "nonexperts" in numerous fields, ranging from diamond-cutting to law. They found that there was only one differentiating factor—not intelligence or even hard work, but rather an openness and drive to learn constantly.

Because I thought we should all hold ourselves accountable for achieving results, I wrote "achievement" next. "Efficiency" and "integrity" rounded out my list.

By the time the cab reached my apartment, I was on a high. My thirty-minute ride with my laptop not only was therapeutic for me personally but turned out to be one of the turning points in our development. Over the next weeks I would engage our staff in shaping and revising these operating principles. Through this process we added "sense of perspective" and "sensitivity," and we fine-tuned the definitions of each of the principles. This was a critical step in tackling our organizational difficulties, and it was only the beginning.

The Power of Good Management

After several long discussions with our management team, I determined we needed to consolidate. To lower our costs and simplify the organization, I would manage Teach For America and TEACH! myself. Daniel Oscar would leave us to start The Learning Project as an independent nonprofit. Dan Porter would leave the organization to pursue other interests. Richard would assume responsibility for fundraising, the greatest challenge facing the organization.

At the same time that I continued to wear out my welcome with our national funders, Richard quickly diagnosed the problem with our regional fundraising efforts: The regional directors had not committed to secure a certain amount of money, some didn't know how to conduct funding meetings, and sometimes their proposals were poorly written. He clamped down. He worked with the executive directors to establish local goals, he helped them develop agendas for meetings, and he provided feedback on their written proposals. Some felt that his hands-on approach insulted their intelligence. They weren't used to close management. In an effort to be accommodating, their managers had taken a feel-good approach. Richard persisted. He was determined to resolve our financial situation.

Watching Richard, I realized something pivotal: Whether or not Teach For America met its goals would depend on whether or not our organizational leaders—and I myself—were effective managers. It was great to have big ideas. But they wouldn't grow into successful initiatives without effective management at every level. We would need to define goals and hold ourselves and our staff accountable for meeting them. And we would need to invest the energy needed to develop our staff members' capacity to reach those goals. This was a big shift in my thinking.

Richard's efforts began paying off. Our local staff started spending more time raising money. Their lists of prospects grew. They came to appreciate the clear focus and the guidance, and they felt better about their jobs as they became more successful. It was also amazing to me to see that now that our staff had bought into the operating principles, they pretty much followed them. Our organization was starting to become a different place.

Cutting Back

Although our culture started to improve, our financial situation was still dubious. We were fighting to stay afloat. Richard took charge of micromanaging the expense side of the organization. He introduced 8:15 Tuesday morning meetings, where our management team reviewed written requests to make any expenditures. Most of the requests were for amounts ranging from $50 to $200, and most were rejected. Then Richard and Kenji Hashimoto, our level-headed and very organized twenty-four-year-old CFO, would meet daily to review projected inflows and outflows. Working together, they would figure out how to progress on the particular day—what vendors to put off, what funders to call.

We still hadn't missed a payroll. As each two-week period passed, we would raise the money we needed just in time. I would sleep easy for one night and then wake up the following morning already worrying about the next deadline.

It was too late to convince a bank to give us a line of credit. Richard did, however, secure the help of Michael Osheowitz of the Edwin Gould Foundation for Children, which agreed to provide a revolving loan. Each time we secured a written commitment for a grant, the Gould Foundation would wire us the cash for that amount; when we actually received the committed check, we would pay back the Gould Foundation. Once, when we had exhausted every option and didn't even have a future commitment to take to the Gould Foundation, Sue

Lehmann, an independent consultant who had been supportive in the past, wired $60,000 into our bank account about two hours before the funding for payroll was due. We paid her back three days later.

This was too much pressure. We simply couldn't sustain it. One night I met Daniel at my favorite coffee shop, Café Lalo. Our meeting, which Daniel had scheduled to ask for my assistance in raising funds for The Learning Project, turned into a venting session. Over a comforting latte, I told Daniel that I was miserable. He listened sympathetically and then mused that our easiest year had been our first, when we were just recruiting, selecting, training, and placing corps members—before we made our lives more complicated by starting new organizations and providing corps members with an elaborate ongoing professional development program. Good intentions had led us to try to do more, but they had backfired. Maybe, he suggested, we should just go back to what we were doing then and cut out everything else.

I agreed with Daniel: Our first year had been our easiest. But we had come too far; we couldn't just abandon everything else at this point. Our corps members would go back to being unsupported. We would have to lay off half the staff. I would be letting down the funders and staff members who had believed in TEACH! I left Café Lalo and walked slowly down Broadway, contemplating Daniel's advice.

A few weeks later I had dinner with Ian, who had left Teach For America a year earlier to attend Harvard Business School and had come down to New York for the day. I remember our meal as a terribly low point. Absolutely deflated, I suggested that maybe I should close down Teach For America. Ian didn't respond to my thinly veiled request for encouragement; he had seen me encounter so many lows and pull out of them so many times that this conversation probably didn't strike him as out of the ordinary. But this time it was different.

I left the restaurant realizing that I should gather our management team to address a basic question: Should we continue?

The next day I pulled the team leaders together in the national office and asked them that question. An hour into the discussion, Richard took the floor. He said that whatever philosophical issues our critics had, he knew Teach For America was working. During his days as our New York executive director, he used to visit our schools in the Bronx and in Washington Heights. He saw the effect our teachers had in those classrooms. He had gotten to know dozens of principals who told him that we were bringing energy, talent, and dedication to their schools. Also, we were beginning to see evidence that Teach For America was influencing our corps members' career directions. Alumni demonstrated a distinct commitment to working for long-term social change. Six years into Teach For America, we had alumni who were starting schools, pursuing principalships, dedicating themselves to a lifetime of teaching, going to law school to work for educational equity, going to medical school to become pediatricians in low-income areas, and going into corporate America for the express purpose of gaining skills and resources that would ultimately help them make a greater social impact.

The more our management team talked, the more we came back to the original concept behind Teach For America. It might not be what funders thought was "systemic," but it was enormously catalytic. Our corps members were positively impacting the lives of hundreds of thousands of the nation's most underprivileged children. And they were forming a leadership force for the future—a leadership force that would have the insight and commitment to push through the systemic changes necessary to ensure that one day, all children really do have the same chance in life.

Teach For America was trying to do something about the greatest injustice in America: the lack of opportunity facing children born in low-income areas. As long as this injustice persisted, we thought Teach For America should be there fighting it. TEACH! was also a good idea. It was an important effort to address one of the most central challenges we had observed in school districts, the lack of capacity to recruit and develop teachers effectively. But this one initiative wasn't worth jeopardizing the broader movement.

I finally saw what I hadn't seen before—that we did not have the capacity to make two organizations work. We didn't have the people power, the management systems, or the financial resources to run several organizations.

I resigned myself to shutting TEACH! down. We couldn't pursue TEACH! if it meant sacrificing Teach For America. I felt awful about this. It was really my fault that we were in this situation, and I knew that. I had led our staff down this path. I had also convinced some of our biggest believers in the funding community to put themselves on the line by investing in TEACH! But by this point I saw no other option than to let go. I resolved to pursue TEACH! again later, in a different way.

There was one more big decision to be made: We needed to cut our budget. Again, I finally resigned myself to a radical change in my thinking. Instead of figuring out how much we would need to spend and then setting our funding goal at that level, we would figure out how much we could reasonably raise and then keep our costs below that number. Richard analyzed our development history and prospects and came back to us with a revised annual fundraising estimate: $6 million. We would need to trim our budget by $2 million.

The goal was clear. We needed to cut a quarter of our budget without sacrificing our core mission. We considered decreasing the number of corps members, but because our fixed costs were so high, we would need to cut the size of the corps dramatically, by more than half, in order to save $2 million. We considered reducing the number of placement sites but realized that such a move would jeopardize our regional funding possibilities. And I didn't want to cut back on our scale or nationwide scope, as I still felt strongly that these attributes were a fundamental part of being an urgent national movement.

We began focusing attention on our infrastructure for ongoing professional development, which was costing us $2 million. This cut was probably long overdue, not only for financial reasons but for programmatic ones. It seemed that by guiding our corps members' professional development ourselves, we had prevented many of them from taking the initiative to find the support they needed within their schools and communities. When there was a problem, it was assumed that it was Teach For America's responsibility rather than that of the school or school system. And even at a ratio of one to twenty-five, the support directors were unable to provide corps members with all the professional development they needed. We were paying a great deal of money for a program that wasn't working.

At the same time, I had heard that our strongest teachers were finding their own sources of professional development. They were visiting excellent teachers in their schools. They were asking teachers and administrators to observe them frequently—more frequently than our support directors could. They were seeking out the resources they needed in their schools and communities. We needed to foster more of such initiative.

The solution was obvious. The one viable option—and the one we could pursue without compromising our fundamental mission—was to discontinue our effort to provide the corps with this model of ongoing training. Instead, we would foster a support network among corps members and encourage them to take advantage of local resources.

The sad part about this plan was that it meant we would have to let go of our support directors—sixty dedicated staff members. For financial reasons, it didn't make sense to postpone this move: The day the support directors left the organization, our bimonthly payroll would drop from $200,000 to $120,000. But after agonizing discussions, our management team just didn't think it was right to leave our staff members without jobs in the middle of a school year. Ultimately, we kept them on the payroll until the end of the school year, regardless of the continuing financial stress that created.

I decided that we would break the news of our decision about eliminating the support directors' positions on February 21, 1995, the first day of one of the conferences we held three times a year to bring together our regional directors and team leaders for strategy setting and skill building. I figured it would be better to tell the regional directors when they were together in New York, so that I would have a week to address their concerns directly and they could brace themselves for dealing with any fallout.

Standing up in front of thirty or so regional and national staff members, I was nervous. I explained the soul-searching process the management team had gone through in the previous weeks and outlined the course of action we had agreed upon. For the most part, the regional directors seemed to think this was the right thing to do. They sympathized with the staff members whose positions would be eliminated, but they seemed to respect the dramatic steps we were taking. This was what had to happen. This would save Teach For America.

I was relieved, if not a little surprised. We must have made the right decisions if the reaction was this positive. I spent the remainder of the conference week communicating the news internally to the rest of our staff and notifying our major funders and external supporters. The response was encouraging. Our funders and key people in the education community applauded our decision, pleased that we were at last looking to proven institutions to support corps members instead of trying to do everything ourselves. Even a good number of the support directors told me they thought this was a wise move. They believed in Teach For America and were very much aware of our financial difficulties; as much as they enjoyed working with the corps members, they were willing to give up their jobs for the greater good.

The news hit our corps members the hardest. Many took our decision as a sign that we were abandoning them. But I believed our revamped approach would ultimately serve them better.

Planning for the Future

That spring we put a three-year plan into writing. We began by setting an ambitious goal: to turn Teach For America into a stable, thriving institution that could pursue its mission until all children in the United States had the chance at an excellent education.

Then we talked about how we'd meet our goal. We set five major priorities. First, we would gain financial stability. Gone were the days of launching new and expanded programs without knowing where the money would come from. And we would make an aggressive effort to expand and diversify our funding base. We didn't want Teach For America to rely on a few huge grants. That situation was too precarious. We had certainly learned that we didn't have the capacity to run another revenue-generating organization like TEACH! that might cross-subsidize Teach For America. We would be best served by raising our annual budget each year from a great variety of sources.

Second, we would bolster our core programmatic activities, with a particular focus on strengthening the training and support corps members received. Although the summer institute was already dramatically improved, there was more to be done. And we clearly had to create a new approach to ensuring corps members received the support they needed.

Third, we would build our capacity by recruiting great staff members and providing them with effective management and development. I had begun to see the impact of these strategies and was clear that they would ultimately be the difference between a floundering organization and a flourishing one. Fourth, we would strengthen our reputation in the public and in the education community. Fifth, we would strengthen our national board and build regional boards in each of our placement sites. Our experience with Linda Darling-Hammond's article had taught us that we needed allies—respected, experienced leaders who would stand by us. Our organization could not thrive as long as it rested solely on the shoulders of a bunch of twenty-somethings.

Within each of these priority areas, we established concrete measures of success against which we would evaluate our progress at the end of the year. This was another critical breakthrough. We had spent years struggling to develop an effective planning process, creating one form of organizational strategic plan after another. Finally, by focusing on goals rather than processes, we would unleash our staff's entrepreneurial energy. Rather than micromanage staff against process-oriented plans, we would turn them loose to meet defined outcomes. Now our staff had total clarity on where we were headed; all of our efforts would be aligned.

I was excited about these plans. I was sure they would work, if only we could make it through the rest of this school year.

Chapter 7

Reaching the Light
at the End of the Tunnel

With our strategy in place, there were still immense immediate financial needs. Because the support directors weren't leaving our staff until the end of the school year, we needed to continue raising $200,000 for payroll every two weeks through the end of June. Moreover, we had to have enough cash to cover the significant costs for housing, food, and faculty salaries at our training institute.

We were confident about our ability to raise the funds necessary to cover all but about $750,000 of these expenses. Our financial projections showed that if we could find the additional $750,000 by July, we would be home free. After that, thanks to the major budget cuts that would take effect at the end of the school year, we would be on track to financial stability. In fact, our estimates showed that by the end of the fiscal year on September 30, our revenues would actually exceed expenses for the year.

The Hitch

We asked the Carnegie Corporation to host another meeting of funders to discuss our situation. About twenty of the funders who had supported us over time came together in May 1995.

I looked forward to the meeting. Finally, I thought, we would be telling this group of funders what they hoped to hear. We described the lessons we had learned—the need to focus on our core mission, to ensure adequate resources to support our program, to build our organizational capacity through effective management. Then we laid out the funding needs we would face over the coming several months and long-term financial projections illustrating a prosperous future.

Our short-term revenue forecast assumed that the Corporation for National Service would renew its grant. Although the Corporation did not make multiyear commitments, it always renewed grants if the terms of the grant agreements were met. A few months before, a recent law school graduate working at the Corporation for National Service was assigned to be our program officer. Throughout the year, I had called her many times to seek verification that the Corporation would continue its funding of Teach For America. She never returned my calls. I assumed that things were just crazy over there and that everyone was too busy to get back to me. The Corporation knew how heavily we depended on their grant—we were one of their biggest programs—and surely no word must mean that things were on track.

I had sent the program officer an invitation to the Carnegie meeting out of courtesy, thinking I would get no response. So I was surprised when her boss showed up at the meeting. As Richard and I presented our financial projections, this woman raised her hand and asked, "What in the *world* gives you the idea that the Corporation is going to fund you again?" I replied that every AmeriCorps program assumed that its funding would continue as long as it complied with the Corporation's regulations, to which she responded, "Well, you know how many issues we have with Teach For America."

After the funding meeting, Sue Lehmann, the independent consultant who had helped us meet payroll a few months earlier by wiring money into our account, phoned me. She sensed that many of the funders in the room were not convinced of the viability of our plan; she wanted to come by the office to comb through the details of our presentation. As she became convinced that the plan really would work, she grew determined to help us communicate it to the funding community. She wrote a memo to the funders and called them to assure them that we were on the right track.

Rick Love, our program officer at the Knight Foundation, came through for us once again, pledging $100,000 in the form of a challenge grant. We would need to raise $650,000 to gain access to it.

We still had not received any official word about funding from the Corporation for National Service. After the Carnegie meeting, I tried unsuccessfully to contact not only our program officer, but her boss who had been at the meeting and several senior officials at AmeriCorps. None of my phone calls or faxes generated a response. I figured they must understand that the very existence of Teach For America relied on the renewal of their grant. With stakes this high, certainly a potentially negative decision would merit a phone call.

One of the problems was that we needed confirmation of our grant earlier than other AmeriCorps programs did because our corps members began their service in the summer rather than the fall. At the same time, the Corporation evidently had continuing concerns about our financial situation. What I also heard, never directly but through other

AmeriCorps programs, was that the Corporation was unhappy with Teach For America over issues of "national identity." That is, the public knew us as "Teach For America," whereas the public knew other service corps, which didn't exist prior to AmeriCorps, as AmeriCorps programs. This was an understandable concern; a clear identity would help AmeriCorps build support in the public and in Congress. We wrote faxes explaining all that we were doing to promote the identity of AmeriCorps, from including its logo on our stationery and printed materials to using its language on our voicemail systems.

To my great consternation, two weeks before the summer institute in 1995 I still had heard nothing from the Corporation for National Service. In my faxes I had communicated that we needed to have the Corporation's commitment before the University of Houston would let us sign a contract and begin preparing for the arrival of five hundred corps members at the summer institute. I held on to my faith that things would work out because I couldn't imagine that the Corporation would let one of its largest programs go under for lack of $2 million while it dished out millions to other less-proven programs.

One week before the institute, still no returned phone calls. My instinct told me to go straight down to D.C. to knock on the door of the Corporation's chief executive, but again I received word through other AmeriCorps programs that our chances of being funded would only diminish if we sent a fax or left a message for anyone other than our designated program officer.

On Sunday, June 18, 1995, five hundred corps members were scheduled to descend upon the University of Houston. As was the case the year before, our staff members were not allowed on campus to prepare without a funding commitment from the Corporation. So they set up offices in two motel rooms in Houston and did what they could without stepping on campus. As of the weekend before, we had not heard anything. My stomach and chest were tight with stress. I couldn't sleep. Why couldn't the people at the Corporation just make the single phone call that would explain what was going on?

For the first time in six years, I contemplated the possibility that Teach For America would not make it, despite all the steps we had taken to stabilize the organization, despite all we had learned and done over the past several years. I imagined what we would have to do: If we did not hear from anyone on Friday, we would Federal Express notices to corps members that the institute had been canceled because of lack of funds. After that, we would lose the confidence of college students and funders. We would be through. How ironic it all was! Through their own inaction, the officials of an agency whose mission was to develop new national service programs would destroy a model that had proven its success through six years of experience.

Monday and Tuesday passed with no word. On Wednesday I received a phone call from our program officer scheduling a conference call for Thursday morning. I couldn't imagine what they were going to say. The conference call was excruciating. Six Corporation staff members explained that they would renew our grant only if we met two conditions. First, we had to agree to accept "education awards" for our corps members. Second, we had to cut another $1 million from our budget by the following day.

I couldn't believe the paradox of these two conditions. All other AmeriCorps members received education awards, which could be used against any past or future educational expenses and were worth approximately $5,000 per year of service. But unlike our teachers, other AmeriCorps members were making small stipends rather than full salaries. We had survived just fine without this federal expenditure of $5 million a year. (Any new teachers in certain low-income areas, including our corps members, already qualified for loan forgiveness through other federal provisions.) We were worried that the awards would create political difficulties for our corps members, who would be teaching next door to other new teachers who made the same salaries as our corps members but wouldn't receive the education awards.

We were never told why we were being forced to accept these awards; ultimately we gathered that Corporation officials thought it was part of promoting AmeriCorps' national identity. Also, there was plenty of funding designated by Congress for these awards, whereas the funding earmarked for program support was much more limited. Whatever the explanation, here they were requiring us to cut our general operating budget by $1 million while giving us an additional $5 million for something we felt wasn't essential. How did that make sense? But with only two working days before the institute was to open, we had no time to fight. I swallowed my anger, agreed to accept the education awards, and determined to slash another $1 million within four hours. This I did mostly by decimating our recruitment budget, the only thing left to cut.

At long last, at 4:45 on the Friday afternoon before the Sunday corps members were expected to appear on campus, a senior official at the Corporation made a call to our contact at the University of Houston. Our staff was finally allowed on campus to begin preparations for registration. For the second year in a row, we would run an institute for five hundred corps members with just a few hours to get ready for their arrival.

For weeks after this incident, I spent my morning runs scheming about ways to get back at the Corporation for National Service. It was only many months later that I realized that this incident really wasn't about the Corporation. It was about a few individuals in Washington who may have been following their regulations but hadn't understood how lack of communication and inaction would impact our fragile organization. (Incidentally, Teach For America subsequently developed a very good relationship with the Corporation, thanks to the understanding and hard work of a new program officer, Marlene Zakai, who was assigned to us immediately following this episode.)

Meeting the Challenge

Now it was just a matter of raising the $650,000 needed to meet the Knight Foundation's challenge. I secured several pledges totaling $500,000. This left us $150,000 short.

The next week our local directors gathered in Houston for one of their weeklong conferences. At the beginning of the week, I honestly didn't see how we were going to make it. We were so close and yet so far. I had already called everyone I knew, and I just didn't see where these funds were going to come from. The stress was so great that at one point I broke down in tears in front of the group. It was probably the only time I had ever appeared anything but confident in front of our staff. And it probably did more than anything I could have said to cement the loyalty of the group. Greg Good, who was leading our efforts in Los Angeles, pulled me aside and said he wanted me to know he would go to war for Teach For America. Abigail Smith, our regional director in Washington, D.C., wrote me a note about how she had cried in front of her first graders during her first year of teaching.

By the last day of the conference, I had pieced together five more grants for a total of $50,000. We still had to come up with $100,000.

The previous April I had received a phone call out of the blue from Karen Greenberg, who was president of the Open Society Institute, George Soros's foundation that at the time supported only international projects that promoted democracy. Karen, a former Yale professor, had read Linda Darling-Hammond's article in *Phi Delta Kappan* and was so outraged by its faulty research that she wanted to help us. I explained our financial problems to her, and she said she would try to make a grant through Open Society, which had plans to begin funding domestic projects. Finally Karen said she could make a $75,000 grant if we could pull together the rest of the money we needed. Amazingly, the article that Linda Darling-Hammond hoped would put us out of business had rescued us instead. Now we were just $25,000 short.

But I had nowhere to turn. I had squeezed every drop out of my contacts. I began calling some of my colleagues in the nonprofit world, one of them being Bill Shore. He had founded the hunger relief organization called Share Our Strength, and he responded to my call by lobbying the board of the Echoing Green Foundation to come through for us one last time. At noon on the last day of the conference, Ed Cohen, the head of Echoing Green, called me to pledge the final $25,000.

I went down to the cafeteria in search of someone to tell. Our local directors were gathered at a table. "We just got the last grant," I told them. They erupted into applause. They stood; they laughed; they cheered; they shouted. We had made it.

On the last day of the fiscal year, September 30, 1995, AmeriCorps sent us $1 million of the grant they had committed to us. As promised, we finished the year with a surplus. Our revenues actually exceeded our expenses. I felt as if the world had been lifted from my shoulders.

In my internal newsletter column to the staff after that week, I thanked our incredible team for their understanding and flexibility, "for doing things better than we've ever done them despite non-existent resources." I singled out the finance team for special acknowl-edgment, citing their "toughness, patience, faith, and sense of humor." I continued: "Thanks to all of our hard work and persistence, today we enter a new era. The challenges ahead are just as great as those we have already conquered—but they will be the challenges of building an institution and not of struggling to make the next payroll."

I couldn't regret too deeply the choices I had made over the previous few years. There was no getting around that I was who I was then, with the experience I had to that point. If at the time I had under-stood the importance of ensuring the necessary funds before moving forward with new ideas, Teach For America would never have been born in the first place.

From my vantage point, we had always tried to do the right thing. We responded to problems with concern and empathy. Our corps members told us they felt unsupported, and so we built up our local professional development program—a course of action that everyone from our board to our funders had encouraged. Then we saw that Teach For America alone couldn't solve the problems facing school districts, and so we launched a systemic initiative—something, once again, that our funders encouraged. We observed and listened and responded.

In hindsight I came to understand that my greatest advantage was also my greatest disadvantage. My inexperience in the world enabled me to dream up big ideas and pursue them relentlessly. But I was un-sophisticated in my approach to generating the financial support and organizational capacity that was ultimately essential to our success.

As difficult as these years were, they were also very productive. They resulted in two organizations that are still thriving today. The Learning Project, still under Daniel Oscar's leadership, is managing charter schools in New York City and New Jersey and ultimately plans to do so all across the country.

TEACH! is now a separately incorporated organization. In 1997, once Teach For America was on solid footing, I secured a grant to hire Michelle Rhee, a Teach For America alumna who was graduating from Harvard's Kennedy School, to develop its new business plan. Michelle determined that the best way for our organization to have a truly systemic impact was to be a consulting firm that would help districts and states develop the internal capacity to recruit, select, train, and support new teachers effectively. We renamed the organization The New Teacher Project and began consulting in 1998. By 2002, under Michelle's leadership as the organization's chief executive, The New Teacher Project was fulfilling twenty-five contracts with school systems and state departments of education across the country. It was helping clients improve the recruitment and development of education majors, and it was providing cities like New York City, Washington, D.C., Atlanta, Kansas City, and San Jose, California, with more than a fifth of their new teachers through high-quality alternate routes into teaching for young professionals, mid-career professionals, and recent graduates of all academic majors. The New Teacher Project's initial contracts included the creation of the highly publicized New York City Teaching Fellows, which in 2002 attracted 13,000 applicants for 2,000 spots in the city's lowest-performing schools.

These years taught me important lessons, too. First, they taught me about the power of Teach For America's mission. Although I believed in the idea from the start, I got sidetracked when I began thinking about the size of the challenges in education. Ultimately, I had come back around to see that Teach For America is an essential force as long as there is inequity in education. In addition to helping children growing up today, it was generating a body of civic leaders committed to change. What these people would accomplish over the long run would be far greater than I could accomplish by fashioning new initiatives.

I also learned how critical it is to ensure that, as Nick Glover had tried to tell us, the program and fundraising sides of the organization are in balance. It's not possible to sustain ideas if you don't have the money to pay for them. At the same time, I had learned the benefits of thinking strategically about where to spend limited resources. Our program became stronger when we were forced to make tough financial choices.

Perhaps most important, these years told me that the only way to carry out our mission was through the hard work of building an effective organization. Teach For America would reach its potential only if I learned how to be a good manager. And I learned a great deal about how to do that—about the importance of surrounding myself with a talented team, working with them to set clear goals, and growing their capacity. I learned about what I valued in staff members and how to create a culture that fosters those values.

What I learned, in essence, was that if I was to fulfill my mission, it would take more than an idealistic vision. In the end, the big idea was important and essential. But it would work only with a lot of attention to the nuts and bolts of effective execution. This lesson would enable me to strengthen Teach For America in the years to come. It would also factor prominently in my thinking as I gained more time to reflect on what was differentiating our most effective corps members and alumni and on what it would take to build an education system that offers all children the opportunity to fulfill their true potential.

Chapter 8

Upward Spiral

y the fall of 1995, our sixth school year, two generations of staff had come and gone from Teach For America. First there were the people responsible for creating Teach For America during years one and two, most of whom had intended to work with us for about six months and wound up leaving two to four years later. Most of the second generation, those who ran the show during years four and five, had also moved on to other jobs. Richard was the only person who had played a central role in our start-up and was still working with me through this past rough year. But in the fall of 1995, when he was certain Teach For America would survive, he, too, left, to work for a company that aims to improve education.

I felt a little lonely in the first few days after Richard left, but soon I was surrounded by a tremendous new leadership team. Most of these people had come onto our staff at some point during the last extraordinarily difficult year. We were bonded together in a common mission: never again to experience such stress. We were going to build Teach For America into a stable, thriving institution.

Iris Chen, a member of our first corps, assumed the position of Vice President, Program. Iris had written me some long memos about all the problems with Teach For America when she was a corps member. I invited her to come help do something about them.

At the age of twenty-four, Iris was responsible for overseeing our nationwide efforts to recruit, select, train, and support corps members. She supervised, directly or indirectly, three-quarters of our staff. Any normal person with only three years of experience out of college would have balked at this challenge. Luckily, Iris was no normal person. This was a woman who ran the 1997 New York City marathon with mononucleosis, whose belief in our operating principles was so great that she used them to grade her boyfriends, and whose penchant for ironing out our organizational imperfections in long, detailed, perfectly written, and perfectly logical memos led her colleagues to wish her farewell three years later by unscrolling a twenty-three-page memo lauding all that she had done for Teach For America.

Iris was joined in the national office by stars such as Karolyn Belcher, another dedicated member of our first corps, who ran our training institute three years in a row. This was a record. Hers was evidently such a harrowing job that each of the five previous institute directors lasted only one year. Julian Johnson brought twenty years of experience in the field of development, which never prevented him from rolling with Teach For America's energetic, youthful culture. Christine Thelmo, a Princeton graduate who had begun as a temporary data enterer in our second year, had proven such dedication and attention to detail that she became our vice president of communications at just about the same time Richard left us.

Our local offices were also blessed with a cast of talented characters. There was Greg Good, a Teach For America alumnus and former football player from Brown whose movie-star looks, charisma, and love of life put Los Angeles in the palm of his hand. There were Roger Schulman in Baltimore and Eric Weingartner in New York—two burly guys, also alumni, whose warm personalities helped make us a kinder, more fun-loving organization. There was Lara Sellers, a Stanford graduate and former head coach of the women's volleyball team at Colorado College, who turned around our office in the Bay Area. There was Sarah Usdin, an alumna whose outgoing personality and commitment to our mission won the support of the highest-ranking business and governmental leaders in the state of Louisiana. There were many others, all of whom shared a passion for our mission and many of whom had seen it play out as corps members.

Determined to complement our staff with an effective national board, I asked many corporate executives to serve as chair of our organization. I slowly discovered that they were all overcommitted to other organizations. Emerging from its depression era, Teach For America wasn't exactly irresistible. Finally, two executives suggested that Sue Lehmann would be the ideal person.

An independent consultant, Sue works with Fortune 500 companies such as IBM and American Express as well as clients in the foundation and education communities. Among other things, she had helped design AmeriCorps and had advised the New York City Board of Education in its reform of special education. Moreover, having been a student at the University of Michigan when John Kennedy announced his intention to create the Peace Corps, Sue was drawn to the spirit and ethos of Teach For America. She had already demonstrated her belief in the organization, and her willingness to allocate the time and energy necessary to be the kind of involved board chair we needed.

Sue is an energetic, fun woman—always on the move, full of ideas and a lot of spark. I went to her Central Park West apartment and asked if she would take on the challenge of leading and building our national board. She wasn't sure she was the right person and told me we might be better off with a corporate chief executive. I told her that I had come to believe that we needed someone dedicated to our mission who was willing to invest time in it. Given her past support of Teach For America, I was convinced she was the right person. She agreed to think about it. Finally, a couple of weeks later, I had my board chair.

Sue worked with me to recruit seasoned corporate executives and educators who could help us with two of our most pressing organizational needs, funding and marketing Teach For America to college students. While we were strengthening our national board, our executive directors were working to build local boards that could help to raise funds in our regions, increase awareness of Teach For America, and access resources for supporting our corps members in their classrooms.

My Focus

Coming off of the dark years, I resolved to concentrate more on our organization's internal affairs. I dove in enthusiastically, convinced that building effective management systems within Teach For America was the key to fulfilling our mission. Whereas initially I had balked at devoting any time to building a staff, now I reveled in figuring out how to ensure capable leadership throughout the organization. I developed a more involved selection process for staff leadership positions to identify those candidates who shared our values. Using our operating principles as a framework, I tried to see where our staff members were excelling and where they could be even better. And then, rather than shying away from direct discussions, I began seeking them out. I now managed directly a national team of seven people and our thirteen executive directors. I spent an immense amount of time conducting performance evaluations for each of the twenty people. As I began prioritizing these things, the other managers in the organization did the same.

My days were filled with meetings. There were twenty meetings to agree on annual measures of success for my seven national direct reports and thirteen executive directors. There were twenty meetings to decide on budgets, twenty annual midyear reviews, and twenty year-end performance evaluations. There were weekly meetings with each of my seven management team members where I tried to be a resource to help them meet their goals. There were three weeklong conferences where our local executive directors and management team shared best practices and strategized around challenges.

There were cross-team meetings to think about programmatic strategy or organizational initiatives like increasing staff diversity. There was still a regular stream of external meetings, followed up by letters and proposals, as well as frequent trips to regional sites where executive directors would line up fundraising meetings, visits to classrooms, talks with corps members, and events to cultivate potential donors and local board members.

The stream of phone calls and meetings generally lasted until eight at night. By that point I was too exhausted to be clear-headed or efficient enough to spend another four hours doing other tasks, such as writing letters and memos or creating meeting agendas. So I began waking up between three and five in the morning, working until 6:00 A.M., taking a half-hour run, and then working pretty much straight through until ten or eleven at night. I realized that I actually loved getting up, making a hot pot of strong coffee, and then having a few hours of peace and productivity before the day began.

Once our financial situation was a little more under control, I resolved to visit our corps members' classrooms more often. I realized that only if I got out and saw how Teach For America played out in schools would I be able to provide the kind of programmatic leadership Teach For America needed.

In the three years that followed, I visited hundreds of classrooms. I learned a great deal from our teachers (as I describe in more detail in Chapter 10). I also learned more about the impact Teach For America was having and the needs it was addressing.

One of my first such trips was to the Mississippi Delta. A different corps member hosted me each day of my weeklong visit. When I arrived on Monday night, I drove to a house that three of them rented. I was greeted by twenty or so corps members who had gathered in the sparsely furnished house in remote rural Mississippi. These corps members evidently came together in this house quite a bit; the single item in one of the rooms was a copy machine—a real, four-foot-tall copy machine leased by Teach For America that all of the corps members shared. I remember wishing that the rest of the world could have a glimpse of this scene—all these articulate, energetic recent grads, talking intensely about the trials and victories of teaching in one of the most neglected areas in the nation.

During that week I visited nineteen schools in eight different areas of Mississippi and Arkansas. I observed corps members teaching math, French, history, art, English, and science. I observed elementary, middle, and high school classes. Our corps members' students and their parents told me about the challenges they faced, their goals, and their perceptions of the schools and teachers. Principals and veteran teachers told me about the role of Teach For America and about what our corps members brought to their schools. At two potluck dinners corps members shared their experiences and reflections. That trip left me with tremendous respect for corps members in the Delta, who I felt were some of the hardest-working, most compassionate, most dedicated people I'd ever met.

A few months later I took a similar trip to Louisiana, where I visited schools in Baton Rouge, New Orleans, East St. John's, and some of the southern rural parishes (Louisiana's term for districts). Louisiana is one of the few areas of the country where we place corps members in special education classes despite our own misgivings. It takes more training to be an effective special education teacher, but school systems are desperately insistent that we help in this critical area. In one school I visited in East St. John's, the principal had hired all six of his special education teachers from Teach For America.

At another school in East St. John's, ten corps members had developed and implemented a new system for mainstreaming students with behavioral disorders. One corps member had secured computer equipment for the school and then worked with the others to network the computers. When the principal wouldn't let the corps members network the computers from the trailers where they taught to the main building because it would require breaking up the concrete sidewalk, two of our corps members dug ditches to run the wire underneath the concrete. Then the corps members computerized their students' individualized educational plans that are required in special education. When the parish declined to pay the $15,000 for the software, the corps members researched the matter, found out that all parishes had federal funding specifically allocated for the purpose, and after presenting that information, won their funding. Though they made up only about 10 percent of the school's eighty faculty members, the corps members ran 40 percent of the school's extracurricular activities. They started a soccer team, and they won a contest sponsored by Coca-Cola and took fifty students to the Superbowl.

A trip to the Rio Grande Valley left me similarly impressed. At one school I saw a corps member teaching her third graders how to tutor second graders in reading. She taught them how to be "active listeners" and how to ask thoughtful questions. I was amazed to see the third graders follow her advice. There were pairs of little people all over the room, second graders looking up to third graders and third graders intent on teaching their "students" well.

I visited an inspiring alumna, Lillian Quesada, who was in her fourth year of teaching in the Valley. During the half hour I was there, a kindergartner led the rest of the class through the routine of singing the alphabet while Lillian played the guitar, counting, figuring out how many boys and how many girls were in the room, and saying the days of the week in Spanish and English. I asked Lillian if she was working toward a specific goal, and she responded that her goals had changed over time. Her brother-in-law had also come to the Valley and was teaching in a local private school. When she learned that the kindergartners in his school were reading by the end of the year, she realized that she needed to accomplish the same thing. What Lillian told me ultimately led us to encourage our corps members to benchmark their expectations by comparing their own students' performance levels to those of students at schools that are widely regarded as excellent. This proved to be a great way to foster a culture of high expectations in the corps.

In the Rio Grande Valley, some of our corps members had become frustrated that their students, who they felt had tremendous potential, didn't expect to pursue higher education. So the corps members went out and met with groups of parents to educate them about college and how to plan for it.

Without exception, the school principals I met on that trip raved about corps members. One told me that the corps members always arrived before anyone else, that they had great self-confidence because they knew they could be doing lots of other things, and that they brought a needed different perspective because they had come from other parts of the country.

My trips left me convinced that we had to pursue our work with even more conviction and energy, not only because Teach For America was working but because the need for it was so great. In Phoenix, schools struggled to meet the demands created by the constant migration of non-English-speaking families to the area. In one seemingly well-run middle school, seventh and eighth graders read at a second-grade level. A return visit to the Mississippi Delta in the spring of 1998 left me similarly overwhelmed by the need for Teach For America. After the start of the year, there were still more than one hundred vacancies in the fifteen schools where we place corps members. The state supervisor of Mississippi's Tunica County schools told me that high school graduates were regularly hired as teachers in Tunica.

While I saw Teach For America's immediate impact play out in schools, my travels across the country also gave me a glimpse of its long-term impact. Once I went to Austin, Texas, to speak at a reception hosted by the parents of one of our corps members. We had invited our alumni who were in Austin to attend, and when the time came to introduce themselves, one after another cited Teach For America as the most influential experience of their lives. Arti Singh said she would not be in education if it weren't for Teach For America and described her graduate work in education at the University of Texas, where she was focusing on expanding the use of technology in schools. Suzanne Lynn told us how Teach For America had propelled her to become the executive director of Austin's Boys and Girls Club. Everett Volk, who was attending public policy school at the University of Texas, said that because of Teach For America he had decided to focus on community development. Steve Ready moved from the Rio Grande Valley to Austin to continue teaching and was in his sixth year in the classroom; he had brought along one of the students he had taught in the Valley, Juan Orozco, who was attending Austin's St. Edward's University and told me to watch for his application to Teach For America in three years.

The ten or so alumni we had gathered in that room assured me that many more Teach For America alumni were congregating in the state's capital. Many were attending University of Texas graduate schools or working in education. Among others, Dan Davis was the assistant principal of Kyker Elementary, Ben Kramer was the assistant principal of Hill Elementary, and Dan Barkley had worked together with three other people to start a new middle school.

I was amazed that a mere nine years into the history of Teach For America, I could see our impact in a midsize American city—a city where we didn't even place corps members. In Austin I saw that Teach For America was in fact providing communities across our nation with citizens who were more informed and more likely to be engaged in improving their schools and communities.

More Money

With strong local executive directors committed to meeting concrete
funding goals, supported by a national team, our fundraising efforts
took off. In 1996 we covered our operating budget as well as our
$660,000 of long-term debt. Our local executive directors exceeded
the goals they had set, raising $3 million, which was half of our
budget. Another $1.25 million came from the Corporation for Na-
tional Service. National corporations, foundations, and individuals
donated the remaining $1.5 million.

One success led to another. Right before our financial turnaround,
I had met Edith and Henry Everett, a wonderful philanthropic couple
in New York City who are determined to use their resources to fight
some of our country's most pressing social problems. At that time I
was in the midst of trying to find the $650,000 I needed during that
last difficult summer. The Everetts were instantly supportive, even as
other funders who had known me a lot longer were still skeptical
about our plan for gaining financial stability. They called me from
their summer vacation to pledge their help. Now I wanted to start an
endowment to help ensure our longevity and prove that we were in a
new era financially. Over lunch I asked the Everetts if they would consider donating the first million. Henry congratulated me on getting up
the nerve to make such an ambitious request. A couple of weeks later,
he called and made the commitment.

And once again, we finished the year having raised more than our
goal. Our local fundraising efforts were even more successful, and we
closed 1997 with another surplus, some of which helped build our operating reserve and some of which went to a long-overdue investment
in new computers. After moving our office from donated space to do-

nated space for several years, we finally rented a permanent office in the garment district on Thirty-sixth Street between Eighth and Ninth Avenues. We were the first office in this building. We gutted the space, built some fiberboard cubicles on top of the concrete floor, and painted the walls white. When John Pepper, CEO of Procter & Gamble, came to visit us a few months after we moved, he commented, "Well, one thing is clear: You're not wasting any money on your office space." It was a little too bare-bones for some, but I thought it perfectly reinforced our open culture and ideals. Our focus was on our mission and not our surroundings.

Our new financial position gave us more time to think creatively. One result was an event called Teach For America Week. During a particular week each fall, we would invite hundreds of successful Americans to teach in our corps members' classrooms. We thought this idea was a stroke of genius. The event would make influential people all across the country aware of our mission while also generating media attention. And the guest teachers would have a positive impact on the students they taught, particularly since our corps members would be able to prepare their classes and reinforce the guests' messages after they left.

The fall of 1997 saw the first Teach For America Week. One hundred and fifty successful Americans were signed up, including Clinton's Secretary of Health and Human Services, Donna Shalala; former Secretary of State George Shultz; actor Andrew Shue; former New Jersey Governor Tom Kean; Clinton adviser George Stephanopoulos; and commentator Cokie Roberts.

Our board member Sherry Lansing, chief executive of Paramount's Motion Picture Group, had convinced Henry Kissinger to participate. He was slated to teach first thing Monday morning in

New York City. As the time drew nearer, I began wondering whether he and the students would enjoy this. Maybe this wasn't such a good idea after all. But my fears disappeared when I arrived, on time, to find Dr. Kissinger in the principal's office at New York's Intermediate School 164, eating doughnut holes and chatting it up with our New York executive director, Cami Anderson. Dr. Kissinger proceeded to teach in not one but two classrooms, describing how he had escaped from Germany just before the Jews were persecuted, moved to an overcrowded apartment just a few blocks from the school in Washington Heights (where his ninety-seven-year-old mother still lived), and knew no English but learned it quickly in order to survive. He told his class what it was like to win the Nobel Prize and to be secretary of state. Kissinger took a real interest in the students as individuals, asking their names and where they were originally from. "D.R.? What do you mean? Oh, the Dominican Republic! Yes, I know it well. I go there every year to visit my good friends. Do you know of Oscar de la Renta? I go there to celebrate the holidays with him." The kids just loved it. And so did he. He even offered to come back, "maybe twice or four times a year."

This event paid off for us. Dr. Kissinger's enthusiasm persuaded Oprah Winfrey to join us the next year. One of our board members invited Leo Hindery, then president of AT&T, to participate; he wrote to us that Teach For America Week was the highlight of his year and offered a $500,000 grant toward our fledgling endowment drive. A year later he pledged $3 million. *Time* Managing Editor Walter Isaacson taught and then agreed to join our board. In subsequent years we would attract people ranging from Mike Ditka, head coach of the New Orleans Saints football team, to professional basketball players Rebecca Lobo and Hakeem Olajuwon, from Clinton Press Secretary

Mike McCurry to *Today Show* weatherman Al Roker, from Mayors Anthony Williams and Richard Riordan to the chief executives of companies such as Continental Airlines, American Express, Xerox, Mobil Corporation, and Hilton Hotels.

It was an upward spiral. There were further revenue surpluses in 1998, 1999, and 2000. The extra funds we raised went into an operating reserve to help us weather unexpected downturns. Our endowment grew. And we gained the confidence to increase our expenses again. We brought salaries closer to market rates, augmented staff in regional offices, expanded our national communications team, reinstituted the financial aid program that helped corps members make the transition to their new jobs, and invested more in travel and advertising for the recruitment teams.

A Better Program

While we made progress on the financial side, we also set out to enhance our corps members' impact. To improve the training institute, we established measures of success for ourselves regarding what corps members should master by the end of the institute in order to impact their students' academic achievement. We began holding faculty members accountable for their progress against the measures and invested more in their training. To help them meet the measures, we developed a new curriculum that provided corps members with more of a road map for success instead of simply exposing them to a variety of strategies for instruction, classroom management, and the like. The institute improved noticeably, as evidenced by the substantial rise in corps members' satisfaction with the training they receive, though as the final chapters of this book reveal our work is still not complete.

We also moved quickly to improve the support corps members receive during their teaching experience. Again, we established performance metrics and set out to help regional offices meet them by facilitating a sharing of best practices. Through one-on-one conversations, small group discussions, and all-corps meetings, local offices would challenge corps members to maintain their high expectations. We would encourage corps members to advance their professional development by reaching out within their schools and communities, as we had seen our most successful teachers do. To provide corps members with greater access to support, we clustered them in schools, built strong relationships with school principals, and formed new partnerships with schools of education.

Through biannual corps member surveys, we collected data about how we were doing. Then our staff reflected on the results and how we could improve. Although corps members were still facing the exceedingly difficult challenges of working in the toughest teaching situations in the country, they did grow more satisfied with the support they received.

At the same time that we were making great progress, we confronted new snarls. Having decimated our recruitment budget, we shouldn't have been surprised when applications reached an all-time low. When the final application deadline rolled around in 1996, not even two thousand people had applied to join the corps, and the number of applicants who were people of color had plummeted from 46 percent to 37 percent.

I had a terrible sinking feeling. Now that we had finally resolved our financial problems, I thought, perhaps college students were no longer interested in Teach For America. Or perhaps we had erred in focusing too little on arguably the most critical aspect of Teach For America: attracting the leaders who would join our movement. I had taken this aspect of our program for granted after the first year.

We jumped into action. Over the next year, Iris and Kaya Henderson, our dynamic admissions director and another Teach For America alumna, set about boosting our recruitment results. Applying what we had learned in other areas of the organization, we restructured our recruitment effort. Instead of fielding eight recruiters from the national office in New York to cover campuses with specified strategies, we established three regional recruitment offices. We identified a director for each office and asked them to set goals for how many applicants and corps members they would find in their regions. Then we freed them up to build their teams and reach their objectives. The structure enabled us to attract better recruiters, increased their accountability, and turned loose their entrepreneurial energy.

Our recruitment staff set about building relationships with influential faculty and college administrators. They also mobilized volunteers—college students, corps members, and alumni—to raise Teach For America's visibility through postering, flyering, visiting student organizations, writing letters to the editor, and speaking at information sessions. In addition, we created a website and developed a new recruitment video. With the help of our national board, we launched a new public service advertising campaign designed by Wunderman Cato Johnson, at the time the country's leading direct response advertising company. (Sue Lehmann had recruited Mitch

Kurz, then Wunderman's chief executive, onto our board.) Jack Haire, another board member who was the publisher of *Time,* agreed to run the advertisements and convince other publishers to do the same.

Applications rose to 2,500 in 1997, then to 2,750 in 1998, 3,000 in 1999, and 4,100 in 2000, even though the job market grew more and more competitive during that time.

It took a lot of work to overhaul each aspect of our program in this way. Iris lived and breathed Teach For America eighteen hours a day, at least five days a week. I still have images of her walking into my office for our meetings, carrying her 8-inch-thick action plan folder and her long list of issues. But it paid off.

A Stronger Organization

Beyond our achievements in fundraising and strengthening the program, one of the most dramatic changes was in our organizational culture. Staff members began feeling more ownership over their positions. They sought feedback that would help them meet their goals. They felt greater responsibility for our success.

They also began seeing Teach For America as a well-run organization and began talking about it as such. This was a far cry from three years before, let alone eight years before. So although we lost stars who felt compelled to return to graduate school or teaching or to try out another sector, we attracted more talented people. When Iris left us to pursue a J.D./M.B.A. degree at Harvard, for example, her replacement was Jerry Hauser, a member of our first corps who had graduated from Yale Law School and served as an associate for two years at

McKinsey & Company. Jerry proved to be such a strong addition to the organization that a year later he became our chief operating officer.

The negativity that had surrounded Teach For America at the end of the "dark years" gave way to an upbeat atmosphere. This was true inside the organization, and the positive vibes rippled outward as well.

In the spring of 2000, I had the opportunity to have dinner with President Bill Clinton along with a group of young leaders in other sectors. The evening was to begin with a brief discussion of issues of concern to us. I was supposed to say a few words about education.

Our dinner was scheduled for the day on which President Clinton would announce his intention to bomb Kosovo. When I arrived, we were informed that Clinton would be making a televised address at 8 P.M. and would join us shortly thereafter. Our group of twenty-five to thirty people sat in the State Room of the White House watching his speech. Five minutes later the President came in, greeted each of us, and then sat down to dinner.

During my allotted three minutes, I spoke about working with students and schools in the nation's most underresourced areas, everywhere from south-central L.A. to the Mississippi Delta to southeast D.C. I said that we had discovered that it is absolutely possible for such schools to put their students on a level playing field with students from more privileged backgrounds. But the only way to truly ensure that all children have the opportunity to achieve is to inspire more determined, talented leaders to turn their attention to our nation's poorest regions.

As I was saying all this, the President was nodding vigorously. Jeff Schwarz, the president of Timberland, closed our program by asking President Clinton for his thoughts about where our group should focus its energies if we really wanted to make a difference for young people. President Clinton stood up and said that the real solution was much as I had said. In the two-hour discussion that ensued, the conversation continually came back to Teach For America or our corps members.

I sat three feet away from the President, awed that this was actually happening. When an aide came in with a call from a world leader, Clinton told our group to "just wait here" and was back in a minute. Then he offered to take us all on a tour of the White House. We were spellbound. Finally, at 11:45 P.M., after a few more interruptions from world leaders and dozens of stories from the President, we stepped out of the White House on a high. To observe President Clinton's people skills and brilliance firsthand was quite an experience. And for me, it was moving to contemplate what this evening said about how far Teach For America had come. As one of the other guests e-mailed me afterward, "That was quite a validation of your work."

Chapter 9

Taking Stock

In May 2000 close to one thousand Teach For America alumni turned out for our Tenth Anniversary Alumni Summit on the Columbia University campus. Whether or not they were working in the field of education, they had come to reconnect with each other and with the vision of Teach For America. Prominent education reformers and child advocates spoke to our group. Then alumni broke into fourteen sessions on topics ranging from economic development to educational technology, community organizing to the role of business in education.

Most of the panelists at these sessions were alumni. In a seminar on achieving excellence in the classroom, alumni who were still teaching shared their strategies for succeeding with students and rejuvenating their own love of teaching. In a discussion on effecting change through social entrepreneurship, alumni who had started nonprofit organizations recounted their challenges and successes. In another session alumni described the different angles from which they were using the law to benefit children.

I sat in the back of the session on public health as Jeremy Tucker, an alumnus who was at Harvard's medical school, moderated a discussion among three alumni: David Gunderson, who was overseeing the allocation of $23 million for tobacco prevention initiatives in the state of Wisconsin; Mary Murray, who was providing technical assistance to violence prevention initiatives in hundreds of school districts, police departments, and community-based organizations throughout the state of Illinois; and Kimberly Singletary, a resident physician who was working in four inner-city emergency rooms in Baltimore, where she frequently cared for her former students and their families. Then I caught the end of the session about school leadership, where alumni who were school principals told of their aims, hits, and misses.

In my day-to-day travels, I would run into alumni doing remarkable things, but it was inspiring to be surrounded by so many talented, passionate people focused on strengthening our nation's most forgotten communities. Teach For America really had worked. We had inspired civic-minded young people to live out their ideals and to dedicate their time and energy—not only during their two-year commitments but also well beyond them—to addressing the root causes of the disadvantages facing poor children in the United States.

Greg Wendt, a member of our board of directors and a senior vice president of Capital Research Company, stopped me between sessions. He said he now understood the power of Teach For America. He had been sold before, by the idea of providing students with talented teachers. But he couldn't get over the potential of this alumni group. "These are incredible people," he told me over and over. "This is a powerful thing."

Immediate Impact

More than 30,000 individuals had competed to be part of Teach For America in our first decade. Those who were selected and ultimately placed—more than 5,000 of them by the time of the Summit—were people who came to us already having demonstrated leadership and achievement. More than 85 percent had held leadership positions on their college campuses, their average GPA hovered around 3.4, and their average SAT score (self-reported after matriculating) was over 1250. The corps members were a diverse group; as of 2000, 41 percent of those placed were people of color and more than 20 percent were math, science, and engineering majors.

Corps members had excelled in spite of the persistent challenges of adapting to new environments and of climbing the steep learning curve inherent in becoming effective teachers in low-income communities. Their principals had fallen in love with them and fought to hire them. During our tenth year, I began hearing story after story of schools where we had been able to cluster corps members in significant numbers over time and where principals said corps members had measurably increased the schools' effectiveness.

In Donna, Texas, a small rural town in the Rio Grande Valley just about one and a half miles across the border from Mexico, a school called Runn Elementary serves one of the most impoverished communities in the country. Only 10 percent of the parents of Runn's students have graduated from high school, many of the local homes do not have running water, and 88 percent of the students are still learning English. Runn's principal, Ofelia Gaona, has received national recognition from newsman Dan Rather among others for turning the school around. When Ms. Gaona became principal, 5.9 percent of the students (that is, two of them) were passing all of the state's standardized tests. Five years later 80 percent of the students were passing all the tests, and Runn was among the schools designated by the state education department as "academically recognized." Ms. Gaona told me that Teach For America had been one of the major factors in the school's tremendous progress. Our corps members, she said, were always the last to leave for the day, at seven at night, and corps members jumped over the five-foot fence around the school every weekend for six months in order to work in their classrooms until she finally broke the district policy to give them their own sets of keys. "They work hard on the academics," she told me, "and they do it with such caring and love."

In Washington, D.C., Cecile Middleton, a forty-year veteran of the public school system who is well known for her success as the principal of Paul Junior High School, created quite a stir when she applied for a district charter. By becoming a charter school, she would free her school from the district's regulations in exchange for accountability for results. Middleton fiercely and publicly defended her decision to apply for a charter against Superintendent Arlene Ackerman, who feared that others would follow Middleton's lead, thus draining resources from the school district. Despite tremendous public pressure from Ackerman, Middleton never came close to giving in and withdrawing her state charter application. But when Teach For America's D.C. board came together to debate whether or not we should place corps members in charter schools, Middleton stood up at the meeting and declared that she would withdraw her charter application if we didn't provide her with teachers. She said she could not be successful as a principal without the eleven corps members and alumni in her school.

In the Bronx in New York, I had visited Glen Bader, the principal of Intermediate School 145, in the spring of 1997. At the time Bader was five years into his tenure as principal. He was known for turning this 1,200-student middle school around. As I stood on the playground with Bader, I realized that he knew the name of each and every student. But despite all that he had accomplished, Bader said that he had not seen his school make academic progress, as measured by the state's standardized test scores. Three years later, I visited Bader again. In the time since my last visit, his school had gone from being one of the lowest-performing to the highest-performing middle school in the Bronx's District 9. The number of students reading on grade level had climbed ten percentage points in three years; of the 350 graduating eighth graders, all but fifteen would get into specialized high schools. Bader, who at the time of my second visit employed nine corps members and six alumni, said many of these changes came about over the previous three years "with the arrival of a critical mass of corps members to inspire their students and the rest of the staff to achieve." He credited the corps members with bringing a focus on academics.

As Teach For America neared the end of its first decade, two independent evaluators were planning studies of corps members' impact on student performance on standardized tests. In the absence of these results, we relied on the assessment of the school principals who had hired corps members. In an independent survey in the spring of 1999 conducted by the research firm Kane, Parsons, & Associates, an average of over 90 percent of principals rated corps members as good or excellent on twenty-three indicators of successful teaching, including achievement orientation and drive to succeed, openness to feedback, choosing effective instructional strategies, creating a classroom environment conducive to learning, and working with other faculty and administrators. Ninety-six percent of principals reported that the presence of corps members was "advantageous" to their schools, with the majority reporting that their presence was "strongly advantageous."

Despite far less than ideal working conditions and the difficulty of relocating to new communities, the vast majority of corps members—between 85 and 90 percent, depending on the corps—completed their two-year commitment to teach.

Leaders for the Future

And our corps members were having a significant impact beyond their two-year commitments. According to an alumni survey conducted in the fall of 1999, almost 60 percent of our alumni were still working full time in education. Thirty-seven percent of them were still teaching and 21 percent were in graduate schools of education, administrative positions, or education organizations. Of the other 40 percent—those not working directly in education—70 percent reported that their full-time jobs related in some way to education and/or low-income communities.

Our alumni were winning the highest accolades teachers can win. Michael Lach, a member of our first corps in New Orleans, won certification as a master teacher from the National Board for Professional Teaching Standards. Many others have been teachers of the year in counties and cities across the country. As just a few of many examples, Virginia Richardson was Baltimore City's 1997–1998 Middle School Teacher of the Year; Alan Giuliani was the 1998 Teacher of the Year in Phillips County, Arkansas; Eduardo McCann was Houston's 1998–1999 Bilingual Teacher of the Year; and Marshall Matson was the 1999 Teacher of the Year for the Northeast Region of North Carolina.

Alumni were also running schools. We knew of forty alumni who were principals or vice principals and dozens more in training for school leadership. They were running some of the most highly acclaimed charter schools in the country, including the KIPP Academies in Houston and the South Bronx, which were featured on the news program *Sixty Minutes* for their success in bringing low-income students up to an academic par with more privileged students. Several alumni were even starting charter schools in rural communities, which find it particularly hard to attract and retain good leadership. And alumni were transforming existing public schools as well. In Compton, California, for example, twenty-seven-year-old Steve Schatz, principal of Laurel Elementary, posted the second highest advance in student achievement in the district in the 1999–2000 school year; his students showed gains of twenty-six percentage points.

Moreover, alumni were advocating for change from outside schools. Some staffed education organizations; others crafted policy for mayors and superintendents; still others ran for public office. As a striking example, alumna Sara Mosle authored a front-page article for *The New York Times Magazine* in the summer of 2000 calling for public recognition of the limits of volunteerism and the need for fundamental systemic change.

When we were expanding Teach For America into Chicago during our tenth year and were having some trouble negotiating the politics of the education community there, we brought together a small number of alumni to ask for their advice. I was amazed and impressed to meet a group that was already playing a critical role in education in the lowest-income areas of Chicago. The group included Dave Wakelyn, who was conducting a high-profile research project in Chicago schools; Kris Reichmann, who was serving as the executive director of a cluster of schools in the North Lawndale community, one of the most economically disadvantaged in the city; Brian O'Malley, who was assisting a number of corporations on neighborhood economic development; Melissa Venekamp, who was doing community organizing; James O'Brien, a Ph.D. candidate working closely with education reform leader and activist Bill Ayers; Travis Richardson, a lawyer; Suzanne Muchin, the executive director of CIVITAS (Oprah Winfrey's effort to raise awareness of the importance of early childhood development); and Colleen Dippel, who was collaborating with schools to implement Project Achieve, a computer-based system that helps principals to manage their schools more effectively.

Midway through this meeting it dawned on me that our alumni would help resolve every problem we faced in expanding into Chicago. They provided guidance regarding the schools and areas of the city where we should cluster corps members. They offered to introduce us to supportive teacher educators, philanthropists, corporate executives, and potential board members. They told us where we could find low-cost office space. There was an assumption that was never articulated but was fully understood; in this discussion every participant cared about only one thing: the welfare of disadvantaged children.

Teach For America alumni had gathered serendipitously in Chicago, but in areas where we had placed corps members for years the leadership group was even deeper. In Washington Heights, a community in New York's Upper Manhattan that is home to many recent immigrants, alumni were working together to effect positive change. For example, Janice Gordon piloted a laptop computer initiative in her classroom, which helped families purchase laptops for each of the children. (Bill Gates himself visited Janice's classroom, and one year she was featured in Microsoft commercials saying, "My kids are powerful.") The district superintendent eventually asked another alumna, Giulia Cox, to expand the laptop program to all the district's schools. Giulia described Janice, Christine Mulgrave, Kevin Kincade, and other alumni as "instrumental in showing the power of the kids and their laptops." According to Giulia, "The project would not have succeeded without Teach For America alums' and corps members' presence, network, and example." And when all other local financial institutions declined to partner with the district to collect and track the funds contributed by the students' families to purchase the computers, Giulia turned successfully to a community-owned credit union in Washington Heights. The credit union, which provides adults and businesses with financial services not otherwise available, had been started by another alumnus, Mark Levine.

In 1999 Teach For America alumni were helping to lead this Washington Heights school district. Judith De Los Santos was the director of bilingual programs, Stacy Douglas was in charge of science education, Yvette Sy was in charge of implementing science curriculum in all the district's middle schools, Giulia was in charge of integrating new content and performance standards into teaching and learning in middle schools, and Christine Mulgrave was the director of the laptop initiative. Out of a district instructional team of about twenty people, Teach For America alumni constituted 25 percent of the decisionmakers and implementers. Although our corps members had initially committed only two years to teach in Washington Heights, many had stayed, and they formed a significant force of young people determined to provide the long-term leadership and people power needed to bring about lasting change in the neighborhood.

.   .   .

Ten years into Teach For America, there was no question that we were having the impact I had envisioned as a college senior. We formed a critical mass of dedicated young people in some of the nation's most underresourced communities. And we were building a force of civic-minded leaders for the future.

Chapter 10

Realizing the Vision

Over time, as I visited the classrooms of our corps members or alumni who were still teaching, I began to see that some of our teachers were in a different league from the others. Most of our corps members are committed, enthusiastic teachers who are excellent by the standards that exist today; as I've said before, their principals rave about them. But I witnessed a few of them attain a whole different level of success.

These are people like Ray Chin, a high school biology teacher in Los Angeles who decided to start an Advanced Placement biology class and coached twenty of his twenty-six students to score a 3 or better on the exam. (A score of 3 out of a possible 5 is considered "passing" on this rigorous exam and often qualifies the recipient for college credit.) Or Amy Black, who had her students in Baltimore City meeting state writing standards for high school graduates by the time they completed eighth grade. Or Trutina Maria Sowell, a first-year corps member in Lynwood, California, who taught twenty-four of her thirty-one kindergartners—most of whom didn't want to be in school on the first day and didn't know how to hold a pencil—how to read.

I wondered what these teachers were doing differently. Why were they so successful? As I visited classrooms, the classrooms of solid teachers and outstanding teachers, I searched for clues.

Aiming to Level the Playing Field

In the spring of 1999, I went to Gaston, North Carolina, to visit Tammi Sutton. Missy Sherburne, the executive director of our rural region in eastern North Carolina, had told me that Tammi, then in her third year of teaching language arts and social studies at Gaston Middle School, had attained phenomenal success with her students. Not knowing much more than that, I flew into Raleigh, rented a car, and drove to this remote little town. I parked in a gravel parking lot and walked into the one-story school where 95 percent of the students were African American, all the students qualified for free lunch, and four Teach For America corps members constituted about a third of the faculty members who were teaching the core academic subjects. The principal, Lucy Edwards, had been named the county's principal of the year twice in a row. Three years before, her school was one of the lowest-performing in the state, with fewer than 50 percent of the students at or above grade level; now the school had achieved an "exemplary" ranking in the state's accountability system. When I talked with Ms. Edwards, she told me the turnaround was thanks to our corps members. Not only did their students' standardized test scores bring up the school's average by thirty percentage points, but the corps members had inspired other teachers to work harder and try new things.

I walked into Tammi's classroom to be greeted by a 5-foot-5-inch woman with short sandy hair, a determined manner, and a rich southern accent. Her students were sitting in groups of four reading a poem Tammi had written called "Twenty Four Years and Learning." As the students helped each other understand the poem, I found myself listening for leads that would take my own interpretation to a higher level. After bringing the class back together and talking through the poem's tricky parts, Tammi handed back poems the students had written in the same format, marked up with her feedback. The students spent time editing and rewriting their poems. Then they read a complex poem by Nikki Rosa, again in groups, and helped each other interpret it.

I watched Tammi teach, talked with the principal and the other corps members, hung out with her students after school, drove them home with her at 7 P.M., and talked with Tammi and other corps members over a chicken tender dinner at a local restaurant. I eventually pieced together the reasons for her success.

Although Tammi's students hadn't been tested the year before, fewer than half of the students in the school generally demonstrated that they wrote acceptably according to the state's standards. Tammi intended to ensure that by year's end they would not only master the technical aspects of good writing but would also be attuned to more sophisticated matters, such as narration, imagery, and style. Tammi set out on a mission to give her students the writing skills necessary for success in high school and college.

Then she went about doing whatever was necessary to invest her students and their families in working with her to reach that goal. She got to know them through church dinners, cookouts, and family trips where she was invited along. She started a Saturday night basketball league. She and another corps member planned an extracurricular trip to Egypt; even though she and her kids only got as far as Orlando, the trip was a bonding experience.

To build a culture in which success and learning were "cool" and where each student felt accountable for and to the group, Tammi often divided the class into groups of four. When a whole group demonstrated superior social or academic skills, it would receive a "superstar group slip." At the end of each grading period, Tammi took the group with the most slips and the most completed homework on an outing of their choice, whether to the state fair or skating or bowling or to the beach.

Tammi constantly reinforced the importance of education with her students. In fact, she got them talking about college. Together with other corps members at her school, she started an extracurricular program to help make students aware of their college options.

With her students motivated to achieve, Tammi taught purposefully. She figured out how to maximize every minute of her class time to work toward her ambitious goals. Landia Dinkins, a seventh grader in Tammi's class, told me that Tammi "really teaches you so you know the answers," that she "gets you thinking" and makes you "feel smarter."

When Tammi discovered that all this wasn't sufficient—that despite her best efforts, there simply wasn't enough instructional time to catch the students up to where they needed to be—she and the other corps members in the school figured out how to make more time. They started Saturday morning tutoring sessions. They actually convinced the principal and other teachers to lengthen the school day by forty-five minutes. They arranged with the principal and the students' families to keep their students in their classrooms working on homework until seven at night.

By the end of the year, Tammi had met the goal by her own assessment as well as the state's: 96 percent of her sixty students performed above state standards for acceptable writing, and many of them performed well above those standards.

In watching Tammi, I realized that she was determined to see our vision—of all children having the opportunity to attain an excellent education—happen in her classroom. Tammi didn't fix on an end goal of building her students' self-esteem or developing their love of learning or building rapport with her students. She may have wanted those things as well, but she knew that if her students were going to have the same chance in life as children born in more privileged circumstances, they would need to gain the same academic skills as these more privileged students.

So Tammi didn't set out to improve her students' academic skills just marginally. Instead, she set out to see to it that by year's end her students were nothing short of fabulous writers. She set standards far beyond gains on standardized tests, but she also used those tests as a quantifiable way to compare her students' progress with that of other students. She wouldn't have been happy with gains of a few percentage points because a few percentage points weren't enough to give her students equal life prospects.

I came to see that a deeply held commitment to realizing dramatic gains in students' academic achievement differentiated our best teachers. I once visited a Teach For America alumnus who was teaching summer school at a school in the Los Angeles Unified School District. His principal gave me a tour of the school and raved about this guy, whom we'll call Joe. Joe was about to enter his fourth year. I walked into his class and was immediately struck by his big smile, his warm manner, and his enthusiasm. Joe clearly loved his kids and loved teaching. But I didn't feel the sense of urgency that was apparent in the classrooms of Tammi or of our other exceptional teachers.

After his students left the room, I asked Joe what it was that he was aiming to accomplish the following year. He outlined various goals he had set for himself. Among other things he hoped to become a better writing teacher by testing some new strategies he had learned in a writing workshop. His answer struck me because his goal was about his own development—becoming a better writing teacher—rather than about his students' achievement—their becoming good writers. We kept talking, and I asked Joe where he thought the kids who would come into his class would be performing when they started the year. He said he couldn't really tell me where they were in relation to grade level because they were so far from grade level. So I asked him what he thought might happen if he just resolved that next year his students would end the year on grade level. Without hesitating, he said, "That would change everything."

Then he started telling me about all the reasons why it wasn't possible. "There's so much that just comes at me that has nothing to do with working toward that goal—so many initiatives and so much paperwork," he said. "Actually, I'd have to rearrange how I spend my whole day. . . . You know, there would just be so many challenges— my kids don't do anything but watch TV all day once they get home." As we tallied up all these hindrances, it was obvious that Joe did think that his students could perform on grade level by the end of the year. The problem wasn't with them but rather with the external barriers that would have to change to enable them to reach their potential.

We talked a little more. We talked about how it would really change his kids' lives if they could get on grade level by the end of the year, that they would really be on a whole different track with whole new worlds of opportunity open to them. We talked about how, as Joe had said, such an ambitious vision would change everything. It would give him the motivation to do something about the external forces that kept him from ensuring his students' success.

It Takes More

Intent on making sure her students achieved excellence on an absolute scale, Tammi recognized that she would have to give her students a lot more—more time, more support, better instruction—than other students might need.

Some believe that if students in low-income areas have hardworking teachers, new textbooks, and well-maintained school buildings—in short if they have the same resources as students in more privileged areas—they enjoy equal opportunity. Yet, although it would be a major step forward for Tammi's students to have access to such resources, Tammi set her bar higher. Rather than measuring her success by whether she provided her students with the same resources as students in other communities, she measured her success by whether they attained the same education.

She knew that her students had the potential to achieve at the same level as students anywhere in the state. Given their *potential* to achieve at the same level, she refused to settle for anything less. To accomplish that, she had to offer her students far more than even the best-financed schools in North Carolina offered and had to do far more than even the best teachers in wealthier communities did.

In higher-income communities, teachers might have the luxury of considering themselves resources from whom students can choose to gain knowledge en route to college. But successful teachers in the low-income communities of Atlanta or East Palo Alto or rural North Carolina view their role in a more active way. Their students generally come to them with significant disadvantages. Most are behind from the day they enter first grade, perhaps because their families didn't have access to good preschool programs or couldn't provide adequate nutrition. As the children grow older, the stresses of poverty make it harder for them to excel academically. In some cases they shoulder heavy responsibilities, such as taking care of younger brothers and sisters while parents work, or they live in communities that are chaotic, violent, and drug infested. Providing children in this context with equal resources clearly doesn't grant them the same education that children in higher-income areas receive.

It's Not Magic

Many teachers come to Teach For America driven to ensure that their students achieve academically in an absolute sense. And yet not all of them succeed. Why? I'll bet many would guess that people like Ray Chin and Trutina Maria Sowell and Tammi Sutton are simply uncommonly charismatic. Yet I have found other factors at work.

We all know the story of Jaime Escalante, the teacher who coached his students in south-central Los Angeles to pass the calculus Advanced Placement exam. Perhaps because Escalante was immortalized in the movie *Stand and Deliver,* people presume that it would be impossible for any mere mortal to replicate his success. We think of him as someone who was born to be a teacher, who had a God-given ability to inspire his students to reach extraordinary levels of achievement.

But what I realized in getting to know exceptional teachers at many grade levels and subject areas—soft-spoken people and loud people, creative people and analytical people—is that good teaching is not about charisma. It's not anything magical or elusive. These teachers set clear goals for their students, motivate people (in this case students and their families) to work hard toward the goals, work relentlessly to accomplish them, and constantly assess their effectiveness and improve their performance over time. As I got to know these teachers, a whole new conception of teaching formed in my head. In our country's lowest-income areas, good teaching was, at its essence, good leadership.

In the spring of 1999, I visited an elementary school in Compton, California, where a number of our corps members were teaching. I observed three first-grade teachers and was very impressed by their rapport with their students, their control of their classrooms, and their enthusiasm for teaching. I was shocked, therefore, when the principal showed me their students' results on a recent standardized reading test. Two of the teachers had effected little or no gains in their students' achievement in the course of a year. But one teacher, Anthony Griffin, had helped his students achieve results that were excellent by any standard. He produced gains of more than thirty percentage points over one year. This compared to the school's average 1 percent improvement in the first grade.

Anthony was a quiet thirty-three-year-old, a former accountant who had come to Teach For America after five years of experience at Price Waterhouse. A visitor to his classroom wouldn't necessarily guess that his results would be so dramatic. His classroom was organized, but his teaching style wasn't particularly dynamic. In fact, a visitor might have guessed the results would be more dramatic in the other teachers' classrooms; on the surface, some of the other teachers seemed more outgoing. In Anthony's class the day's agenda was printed clearly on the board. With very calm directions, Anthony was able to inspire the students to do exactly as they were asked. I observed him reading to the students, asking them questions comparing a book to others they had read, and then organizing the students into "centers" so that some could practice spelling words, some could practice alphabetizing words, some could practice writing, and he could read with a small group.

When I asked Anthony what he thought was distinguishing his performance so dramatically, he told me that he thought it might be his focus on his students' work. He entered the year with a clear sense of what he wanted the students to learn; because he had taught second grade the year before, he began the year thinking his first graders had to end the year at the second-grade level. Each day Anthony would scrutinize his students' work to determine what more he needed to do to help them reach the goals he had set for them.

Like Tammi, Anthony had well-defined targets for his students' performance. His clear, measurable goals drove all of his decisions.

Beyond setting clear goals, our exceptional teachers invested their students in those goals. These teachers generally develop close personal relationships with their students. They spend time with them after school and get to know their families. Building on this base of understanding, they go about convincing their students to believe that hard work will lead to academic success and that academic success will lead to success in life. They expose them to role models who went to college and show them college and job opportunities that open up to them if they work hard.

At the same time, these successful teachers build a culture that advances their efforts. They continually reinforce values such as hard work and teamwork. They set high standards for behavior, not for their own sake but rather to make sure the goals are met. They ask the students to behave so they can succeed both individually and as a group.

Knowing the important role students' families play in determining their success, these teachers go to great lengths to involve their students' parents and guardians in their efforts. They work to ensure families support their efforts in basic ways: by getting their kids to school on time every day, by reinforcing their messages about the importance of hard work, by encouraging them to read, by finding them a quiet spot to do their homework.

With students and families invested in working with them, these teachers are on a mission to move their students forward. A few minutes after entering their classrooms, I always sense something special at work. There is an urgency among students and teachers. With lofty goals for their students, who are already significantly behind, the teachers know they need to maximize every moment. So they choose their instructional strategies purposefully. They take pains to individualize instruction, to ensure that all of their students from the lowest-performing to the highest-performing are learning, to ensure that their students truly understand the concepts they are trying to teach.

These teachers do whatever it takes to reach their academic goals. When they find that there isn't enough time in the day, they figure out how to lengthen it, by getting the students to come early or stay late or attend school on Saturdays or during the summer. When they discover that health issues or family problems are holding their students back, they find social services that can help. When they discover that students don't complete their homework because they can't find people to help them get over tricky spots, they insist the students call them at home for help.

Finally, these teachers are committed to self-improvement. Tammi did not achieve extraordinary results in her first year, but she persisted, reflected, and changed her practice.

After talking with a number of our top teachers, I read an article about exactly how it was that Jaime Escalante achieved the success that he did. Sure enough, he had done all the things I've mentioned: He had established an ambitious goal (ensuring his students scored a 3 or higher on the Advanced Placement exam), inspired his students and their families to work toward it, chosen instructional strategies intentionally, and strengthened his practice through rigorous self-assessment. In short, he did what an effective leader does in any context. Jaime Escalante does not need to be an aberration. It is possible for dedicated, driven people to attain the same results. It's not magic.

Excellent Schools

While I visited corps members across the country, I also had the chance to visit some of our alumni who had started schools, people like Chris Barbic. Chris was one of our exceptional teachers, and the parents of the students he taught petitioned the Houston Independent School District to let him open his own school.

Chris started the YES College Preparatory Academy. In the 1999–2000 school year, 99 percent of YES College Prep's students passed the state's standardized tests in reading and math, and 100 percent passed in writing. In the same year, the YES high school was named the top-performing public high school in the state of Texas based on standardized tests and attendance rates. But YES doesn't rest on these laurels. It pushes its students to surpass the standards of basic skills tests, insisting they meet the criteria necessary to compete for admission at good colleges.

I wondered what accounted for the success of people like Chris, and in the spring of 1995 I set out to find out. I dedicated a day to visiting the KIPP Academy, a school in the South Bronx started by another Teach For America alumnus, Dave Levin.

Dave Levin and Mike Feinberg had joined Teach For America upon graduating from Yale and the University of Pennsylvania in 1992. They were assigned to two low-performing schools in the Gulfton area of Houston. Determined to succeed, they observed other teachers during their lunch breaks. One amazing veteran teacher in Dave's school, Harriet Ball, taught them creative new ways to teach basic skills and critical thinking skills.

In his second year, Dave asked his principal for the lowest-achieving class. On the first day of school, he told his students that he had asked to teach them. Why? Because they were the worst-performing class; 17 percent had ranked at grade level on the state's standardized test. "If you work with me, you'll be the highest-achieving class by the end of the year," Dave told them. At year's end 94 percent of his students scored at grade level.

Mike's story was similar. During his second year, he taught history and math to two classes of students, most of whom spoke so little English that they were exempt from taking the state's standardized tests for reading and math. Of the students who had taken the math test, about a third had scored at grade level before Mike taught them. By the end of the year, the vast majority of the students took the test. Ninety percent scored at grade level.

Dave and Mike didn't think it was enough to achieve these results in two classrooms if their students were going to go on to other classrooms that offered them less opportunity. So they convinced the school district to let them combine their classes into what they called the Knowledge Is Power Program. They recruited students into this program who would come to school at 7:30 in the morning and stay until 5:00 at night. The students, their parents, and the teachers signed a contract committing to meet certain expectations. Dave and Mike brought a high-energy approach to instruction and took the students on trips to reward their effort and enrich their learning. It worked. As one indication of their success, whereas only 62 percent of the students passed the reading test upon starting KIPP, 93 percent of them passed by the end of the year; whereas 60 percent passed math upon entering the program, 96 percent passed math upon leaving it.

On the basis of this success, an education reform group offered Dave and Mike the opportunity to run an entire school in New York City. In an effort to keep them in Houston, the Houston Independent School District offered to let them run a school as well. Mike decided to start a KIPP Academy in Houston, and Dave returned home to New York City to open one in the heart of the South Bronx. It was Dave's school that I visited in May 1995.

When I arrived at 7:30 A.M. at P.S. 156, which housed KIPP, thirty-two of the thirty-nine KIPP students were already sitting at their desks working diligently on a thinking skills worksheet. The worksheet included brainteasers based on math and reading skills, knowledge of geography, and logic. Most of the students had spent the previous week in Washington, D.C., and the brainteasers were all based on their class trip.

"The heat is not going to keep us from thinking," Dave prodded as he walked up and down the rows of bent heads. It would be a ninety-six-degree day in New York, and there was no air conditioning in P.S.

156. Dave didn't miss the opportunity to reinforce the belief that no obstacle was insurmountable, no excuse acceptable. They would work through the heat.

About half of the students had arrived by 7:15, and the remaining seven would arrive before 8:00. When Desiree showed up fifteen minutes late, Dave was after her. "But I woke up at 5:45 to get here," she said. Dave rejected her excuse: "I woke up at 5:15," he countered.

Throughout the day Dave and his fellow teachers jumped on every chance to instill the ethics of hard work and respect for others. Two banners that hung in each classroom captured these values: "There are no shortcuts" and "Team beats individual." Midafternoon, after thinking skills, breakfast, language arts, social studies, science, and lunch, Dave was in the midst of his daily math class. One of the students was playing with popcorn and distracting her classmates. Dave used the occasion to discuss the importance of focus. To drive home his point, he shut the windows, turned off the fan, and told the kids to sit up straight. When I later asked Dave if he thought this was going a little far, his response was, "Unfortunately, life is not easy."

I was struck with the sense of urgency with which KIPP teachers were pursuing their goals for the students and at how engaging and effective their teaching was. "Quality instruction drives the bus," Dave told me. His students agreed with that assessment. Yolanda told me: "Here they make a song up to teach you math. They help us understand more. It's fun. Other classes don't participate like this." Victor agreed: "We learn a lot and it's fun because we learn." KIPP teachers weren't using a single instructional approach. "We're looking for things that work," Dave said. Each teacher selected whatever strategy was most effective in moving the kids forward.

During Dave's math class the students were so engaged that they didn't even realize they were cutting into their time for gym. He had them operating way ahead of where fifth graders were supposed to be. "You guys just did some serious algebra," he said at one point. After talking through one of the thinking skills problems and a lesson on changing fractions into percentages, Dave began a contest. Each of the kids had a small chalkboard, Dave gave them a problem, and they raced to be the first to get it right. "The numerator is 4 times 10 over 20 plus 4. The denominator is 100. What's the percentage?" This contest was so engaging that I found myself competing with the kids. Even the gym teacher, who had come to pick up the class, asked Dave if she could join in.

The teachers' hard work did not stop in the classroom. Teachers visited students' homes virtually every day after school. Students had toll-free numbers for their teachers, which they used when they needed help with their homework or in case of an emergency.

After school ended, I went with Dave and Marina Bernard to visit the home of Zakia, a fourth grader who had expressed interest in attending KIPP the following year. KIPP's teachers go to students' homes before the start of the school year in an effort to convince students and their parents to join the school and sign the school contract. The students who enroll in KIPP aren't necessarily high achievers. Many come with a history of high absenteeism and low grades, but they must all commit to hard work. Parents must promise to make arrangements for their child to attend the extended hours, "to help our child in the best way we know how," and to check homework every night. Students promise to "always work, think, and behave in the best way I know how."

We entered the housing project where Zakia lives and knocked on her family's apartment door. Zakia was a little girl with bright, curious eyes. Her mother was a very young woman who clearly cared a great deal for her daughter. The apartment was small but neat, and a corner was devoted to pictures of Zakia and pieces of her schoolwork. Dave described KIPP to Zakia's mother very simply: "This is a program designed to prepare students for success in high school and success in college." It was clear from her reaction that KIPP's mission resonated with her. After describing all the requirements of KIPP, as well as the benefits, Dave left the family to decide whether or not they would join. He and Marina dropped me off at the subway.

I couldn't stop thinking about what Dave and his colleagues were accomplishing. They were changing the life prospects of the students at KIPP. And over the years I watched KIPP expand so that it was serving several hundred students. As it grew, Dave made it a point to recruit talented teachers; some were Teach For America alumni, some veterans who had taught for years in the Bronx. He also hired an experienced educator to train and develop his teachers by helping them plan their instruction.

KIPP doesn't work because of one unique instructional strategy or cutting-edge curricular model. KIPP's success is the result of a good leader who had an ambitious vision for ensuring that students fulfill their true potential. Dave recognizes that it will take more than what schools typically provide to realize that vision, so he lengthens the school day and steps up student services. Finally, he goes about the tough job of constructing an effective organization. He recruits talented teachers and trains and develops them so that they utilize the same strategies that led to his own success and to the success of any outstanding teacher in a low-income area. And he supports them by creating a schoolwide culture that promotes hard work and personal responsibility.

Educational Opportunity for All

By the time they are nine, children studying math in low-income areas are already one to two grade levels behind nine-year-olds in high-income areas. In reading, they are three to four grade levels behind. And this gap only widens to the point that a child who grows up in south-central Los Angeles is seven times less likely to graduate from college than a child who grows up in Beverly Hills.

Yet Tammi Sutton and Dave Levin and others have shown us that these disparities don't need to exist. We can ensure that children in the poorest communities in America have the same average achievement rates as more privileged children. What I have learned in building Teach For America and from our corps members and alumni suggests that it will take three things to raise achievement levels in low-income schools.

First, it will take committing ourselves to the vision that one day, all children in our nation will have the opportunity to attain an excellent education. We aspire to be the most just, most fair nation, a nation of equal rights and equal opportunity. We aspire to prosper economically and to have a strong democracy. We aspire to be a nation in which universities, Supreme Court benches, and corporate boardrooms are diverse; to be a country of racial harmony; to live in safe communities. If we aspire to these things, then we must address the fact that one's place of birth in the United States largely determines one's educational prospects.

I believe that simply committing to this vision—truly, sincerely committing ourselves to making the odds even for children in low-income areas—will take us a long way. In my first year of Teach For America, I saw the power of a big idea. Later, through people like

Dave and Tammi, I saw how effective the promise of educational equality was in motivating students and their families. I saw how this big mission led teachers and school leaders to do things that normal human beings without big goals wouldn't dream of doing. As our Los Angeles corps member Joe told me, such an ambitious vision changes everything.

Second, we must recognize that accomplishing our mission will take more of just about everything—including more time and, ultimately, more resources. As our corps members and alumni showed me, it takes a lot to help children in low-income communities overcome the disadvantages they bring to school. Providing underprivileged children with equivalent services doesn't get them a good education. It takes more.

Teachers like Tammi are doing more within a system that doesn't provide adequate resources, but it would be unreasonable to expect that thousands of other teachers would be willing to do the same. These teachers work from five or six in the morning until ten or eleven at night, on weekends, and in the summers. They are always on call. To be successful, they are compensating for all the weaknesses of the system in which they work. If the official school day isn't long enough, they devise new structures to add hours. Ultimately it will take more funding to pay for these added services. And if we want our teachers and school leaders to give as much as Tammi and Dave are giving, we'll need to pay them more.

There's an understandable discomfort with the idea that it will take more money to make schools in low-income areas work. We've all seen and read about too many examples of wasted resources in schools. In some cases merely reallocating the resources already spent in low-income areas can make a big difference. And I learned through my experience with Teach For America that money isn't everything, that tough financial situations force high-quality, innovative thinking. But I also learned that although resources are not the solution to everything, they are necessary to carry out big plans.

I'm not saying that schools and school systems can't make any progress without more money. They can. But I don't believe we'll be able to fully realize our vision of educational equality until we as a nation invest disproportionately in education in low-income areas. I hope examples of successful teachers and schools will before long give the public confidence that their increased investment will make a difference, that it will ultimately reduce the other kinds of public expenditures that come about when children are short-changed.

The third aspect of realizing our ambitious vision is the recognition that it will take a long-term, institution-building approach. Building successful school systems is like building successful organizations in any sector. It will take recruiting talented leadership and staff, developing strong cultures, and setting up systems for accountability and continuous improvement. Again, it's not magic. Just as there is no secret shortcut to effective teaching or effective schools, there is no easy way out of the difficult work needed to build successful school systems.

Many advocates for children and school reform argue that parents in low-income areas should be able to choose where their children go to school. By providing parents with vouchers that allow them to place their child in a parochial or private school or in the public school of their choice, we could create a market pressure that would force schools to improve themselves. Whether or not we go this route, however, we will need to engage in the task of creating good options for parents and students. Parents need to be able to find schools that aren't simply producing achievement rates three percentage points higher than neighboring schools but that are truly putting children on a level playing field with children in much more privileged areas.

Other advocates for change feel passionately about certain reforms like smaller class size or bilingual education or technology-based instruction. But when people think about what makes great organizations work, they see it's not a unique strategy. It's that the organizations have built the systems to achieve results, respond to change, and continually improve. In fact, in some cases, one-off strategies dictated from above simply backfire at the local level. For example, mandating that schools decrease class size, one of the more popular reforms at the moment, can sometimes force schools to move students from the classroom of an excellent teacher to the room of an inadequate one.

Having seen firsthand the power of clear outcome goals, I think education reformers have taken a major step in the right direction by calling upon our school systems to produce measurable results. There's certainly a danger in relying on low-level standardized tests as the ultimate bar. Just as we do at Teach For America, school systems and states will need to keep working to refine their measures of success so that the people in schools can align their efforts against what we really want to see happen. But as we work to improve these measures, we shouldn't run from the standards that already exist.

With defined outcomes in place, school systems will need to better their capacity to achieve results. One extremely important step is to recruit and develop people with great care. Many who are working to address issues of teacher quality are focused on increasing teacher certification requirements or improving schools of education. I would instead focus on helping school districts do what every successful organization does. Districts should launch effective campaigns to recruit talented teachers from every high-potential source, select those candidates with the personal leadership qualities necessary to succeed, and orient their new teachers to the district's vision and mission. They should provide preservice training that will give new teachers a solid foundation from which to grow, and over time they should provide support and professional development to help them become more effective.

The districts that follow these steps will improve the quality of their teaching staffs dramatically. Then, to fill principalships, they can turn to some of their most successful teachers, some of whom might well need the challenges of school leadership to persuade them to remain in the field of education. Thus, districts will find themselves with school leaders who have themselves attained significant gains in student achievement, who know it is possible to do so, and who have the moral authority to lead a faculty of other teachers to bring about the same results.

Building effective school systems will not be easy. It will take superior leadership and a lot of hard work. It will require a critical look at all the forces—from how school boards govern to how states regulate—that could prevent school district leadership from taking an institution-building approach. The good news is that there's no mystery about what it will take. The solutions are within our reach.

There are many other changes that would alleviate the pressure on school systems. A change in the economic circumstances in inner-city and rural areas would clearly make it easier for schools and teachers to succeed. Greater prosperity would lead to more jobs and less financial pressure for overstrained moms and dads and guardians. More money would mean more comfortable living arrangements, better health care, and better nutrition. It would mean more resources for better preschools and more supplementary learning opportunities for children.

Barring a dramatic immediate change in the economics of low-income areas, there are improvements in numerous sectors that could make the jobs of schools easier. Better social services, better low-income housing, and universal public preschooling would go a long way.

We should commit ourselves to making these changes happen. And until we do, there is one feasible goal we should pursue: We should build public school systems that have the mission, resources, and capacity to put children born into significant disadvantages on equal footing with other children.

Recognizing the far-reaching changes that would be necessary to realize our vision of educational opportunity for all children only increased my sense of urgency to build Teach For America into an even more effective force. Until these changes happened, we needed more teachers willing to go above and beyond traditional expectations to provide their students with the opportunities they deserved. At least as important, we needed to build a powerful force of leaders inside of education and outside of it, in every sector and at every level of policy, who would have the commitment to effect fundamental change so that the burden of patching a broken system would not fall on the backs of tireless teachers.

Chapter 11

The Decade Ahead

One day in May of 2000, I got a phone call from Scott Hamilton. Scott is about my age, and after holding various positions in the field of education, he was hired by Don and Doris Fisher, founders of The Gap, to manage the creation of their family foundation. Called the Pisces Foundation, this fund would make significant grants to support a few education reform efforts. Scott said that the Fishers were in New York and wanted to meet with me. They were interested in expanding Teach For America and would be willing to put a few million dollars into the effort.

I hadn't received a whole lot of calls like Scott's in my previous ten years at Teach For America. In fact, I hadn't received any calls like that. So I took the subway to go meet the Fishers in their very modest apartment on the East Side of Manhattan. The hourlong meeting was relaxed. Too relaxed. I left disappointed in myself; I had completely failed to keep the conversation on track and to drive home the power of Teach For America.

But a few days later Scott called to say that the Fishers were interested in supporting our expansion effort. He would need a proposal within a month or so.

Through discussions in the next few weeks, our staff rallied to develop an ambitious plan. The opportunity of such significant funding gave us all a new sense of possibility. We resolved to build on everything we had learned over the previous ten years. What would it take, we asked ourselves, to develop a truly effective movement to expand educational opportunity? After much discussion, we set three programmatic priorities.

The first task was to ensure that a significant portion of our corps members achieved at the level of the most successful among them. Tammi Sutton, Anthony Griffin, and our other top teachers had effected dramatic gains in their students' achievement by pushing themselves up steep learning curves. Based on what we learned from them, we recognized that we could accelerate the development of incoming corps members through even more effective training and support. This would have a significant impact on the lives of tens of thousands of students, whose life chances could be improved by having an exceptional teacher.

Ensuring that corps members achieved a high level of success was also important in developing them into effective advocates for systemic change. When they succeeded in closing the achievement gap for their students, corps members came to understand the complexity of the problem and the many dimensions of the solution. They gained not only the insight that enabled them to be powerful advocates for change but also the confidence and the moral authority to insist on change.

The second priority we established was to foster the leadership and ongoing collaboration of our alumni as a force for long-term change. Although we have always assumed that our alumni would achieve important objectives by virtue of who they are and the intensity of their experience, we recognized at the Alumni Summit that we could do even more to support and catalyze their continuing leadership. Alumni left the summit inspired. Several changed jobs within the following weeks because they felt they weren't making sufficient impact. Most left enthused about working with each other more closely. As Jonathan Klein, an alumnus and our Bay Area executive director, said during one of the sessions, "These are the people I want to spend the rest of my life working with." A group of Washington, D.C., alumni decided at the summit to begin meeting regularly to determine how to improve their local public schools; within months, they ran a successful campaign to elect alumna Julie Mikuta to the D.C. school board. So we set out to foster a stronger network among our alumni and to take a more systematic approach to connecting them with ongoing leadership opportunities.

Finally, beyond ensuring the effectiveness of our teachers and supporting the leadership of our alumni, we resolved to make our movement as large as possible. Given the magnitude of the disparities we are working to address, we set out to grow our corps from 1,000 members in 2000 to 4,000 members by 2005. At the same time, given that the disparities affect African American and Latino students disproportionately, we resolved to increase the percentage of applicants who share these ethnic and racial backgrounds.

As I learned in our initial years, we would need to complement these programmatic priorities with institutional ones. We would need to grow our financial base significantly so that we had the necessary resources to accomplish these programmatic goals. And we would need to expand our organizational capacity by strengthening our staff and technological systems.

We worked these priorities into a five-year plan that called for $20 million in up-front investments and an annual operating budget of $40 million, up from $10 million. Through the Pisces Foundation, Don and Doris Fisher offered us our largest private-sector grant ever—more than $8 million over three years—to send us on our way. We more than matched this grant within four months.

Many of the people staffing the foundations that invested in our growth plan were my peers—people who had helped launch Teach For America, our alumni, and other colleagues in the network of social entrepreneurs. For example, New Profit Inc., which made a commitment of $2 million plus substantial in-kind services from its partner the Monitor Company, was founded and run by Vanessa Kirsch, who also founded another service corps called Public Allies. The New Schools Fund was another new foundation, started by venture capitalist John Doerr of Kleiner Perkins Caufield & Byers, which made a substantial grant. Its executive director was Kim Smith, Teach For America's third employee; its second-in-charge was Lisa Daggs, a Teach For America alumna; and its board included our second chief financial officer, Matt Glickman. Another significant contributor, the Broad Foundation, was managed for Eli Broad by Dan Katzir, who had been on Teach For America's staff in our second year.

We managed to secure such significant levels of support in part because we had matured as an organization. We had acquired invaluable experience. Now we knew how to think through what it would take to meet our ambitious goals, we knew how to present our plans in a way that was compelling to funders, and we had a convincing track record. Of course, now we also had the benefit of influential connections that could be made only through time and increased credibility. Whatever the reasons, we were determined to seize the opportunity and poised to advance our movement.

The week after the Alumni Summit, I overheard a discussion among some of our organizational leaders. "You know," someone said, "I looked at the vision statement as I walked into the office this morning. And I realized something. I actually believe it is possible."

In the hallway that leads to Teach For America's offices, a single statement runs down the wall: *One day, all children in this nation will have the opportunity to attain an excellent education*. Teach For America was started in 1990 with a belief that this vision should become a reality. Now, with over ten years of experience behind us, we feel not only that it should happen, but that it *could* happen. Our experience has given us the conviction that our vision is attainable.

And so, knowing that change is possible, we feel a great sense of urgency. We have no choice but to ensure, through our individual and collective efforts, that one day, all children in America have the educational prospects to fulfill their dreams.

Afterword

As Teach For America approaches the midway point of its growth plan, there is tremendous momentum. In spring 2002, 14,000 graduating seniors and recent college graduates applied to join our corps. That's almost three times as many as had ever applied before. Seven percent of Yale's senior class applied. Fourteen percent of Spelman's senior class applied.

Perhaps the economic downturn, and the rise in civic commitment following the tragic events of September 11, had something to do with this increase. Yet whereas other organizations such as the Peace Corps and AmeriCorps experienced increases of 30–40 percent, Teach For America's applications increased 200 percent. Some of the tremendous response must have resulted from our greater visibility and from the increased resources and energy we have poured into recruitment.

And, despite the economic downturn, we are on track to meeting our ambitious funding goals. In 2002 we raised $21 million in annual funding, a record.

As the size of our corps and funding base grew, we also made significant strides in ensuring the effectiveness of corps members and alumni as a force for short-term and long-term change. By pinpointing what differentiated the top performers in our corps, we have been able to refine our selection model and training curriculum. We have also created a stronger network among our alumni. A website enables them to find each other as well as to locate job opportunities, volunteer opportunities, and resources to help them in their long-term efforts. Regional and national summits provide alumni with additional connection and inspiration.

Some people were worried that scaling up might decrease the quality of our efforts. At the outset, Jerry Hauser, who is still leading our staff as chief operating officer, and I felt strongly that growth would help increase quality because it would force us to systematize every aspect of our program. It would also bring additional resources—both financial and human. So far, our prediction has proved right. And part of our programmatic success is a function of the fact that we have attracted a superstar national management team of Teach For America alumni who are drawn by the idea of building Teach For America into an even more powerful force. Among its members are Nicole Baker, a Ph.D. in education from UCLA with years of experience in the nonprofit and education worlds; former White House Fellow and D.C. Young Lawyer of the Year Lee McGoldrick; Rhodes scholar and D.C. school board member Julie Mikuta; and Jonathan Travers, a graduate of Harvard's Kennedy School and former D.C. schools budget director. Every day I am grateful for the leadership these people and others bring to our organization.

As Teach For America grew in size and visibility, we succeeded in enlisting the support of more influential leaders. Laura Bush named

Teach For America one of the five organizations she would support as first lady. She appeared at events across the country, from New York to Los Angeles, San Francisco to the Mississippi Delta, to aid our efforts to expand. In fall 2001, Mrs. Bush taught each of the five days of Teach For America Week in a different city.

Jerry Levin, former chief executive of AOL Time Warner, served as the honoree of our major fundraising dinner in New York; Craig Barrett, chief executive of Intel, and his wife, Barbara, served as our honorees in Phoenix; and business magnate Eli Broad, who had donated $100 million of his own funds to support education reform, served in this capacity in Los Angeles. Each of these respected executives spoke movingly about Teach For America, and in so doing they added the credibility of their support.

Contrast this to only a few years back, when I was desperately searching for a way to make payroll! Having survived the low points, I genuinely empathize with all those new social entrepreneurs out there who are struggling to break through to "the powers that be." Yet at the same time, I am wary of overconfidence. As the experience of the Internet era showed us, what goes up often comes down. And so I try to keep my eye on the challenges of the future rather than the accomplishments of the past.

And for better or worse, there are many challenges to capture my attention. We have new political challenges as policymakers and the media conflate teacher certification with teacher qualification. There are the financial challenges of almost doubling our annual revenue over 2002's $21 million, during this lackluster economy. We also face the challenge of increasing our organization's capacity quickly enough to accommodate 4,000 corps members. Most daunting of all are the continued challenges of improving upon our program to ensure that our corps members and alumni are truly able to fight educational inequality in our country.

All these tasks leave me as busy as ever. What keeps me going is my outrage at the inequities that persist in our country. As a mom now of two little sons, the issue we're addressing is more real than ever before. What would it be like to have to send my sons to schools where the vast majority of kids do not meet basic academic standards? Where even if they were top performers, they would not be as well prepared as even average students in other communities?

Yet for hundreds of thousands of moms and dads in our country today, there is no option. The achievement gap between rich and poor is larger in the United States than it is in almost all other industrialized countries. In ensuring educational opportunity for all, the United States ranks below Canada, France, the U.K., Spain, Australia, New Zealand, Norway, Denmark, Sweden, the Netherlands, Finland, Austria, Latvia, and Poland. As a country that believes itself to be the land of opportunity, we should be outraged by that. To live up to the ideals we hold for our nation, we must do better.

And we can do better. Last spring, Chris Barbic, the alumnus who founded the YES College Preparatory Academy in Houston, telephoned to tell me a funny story. He said he had created a robotics program at his school, a program that is becoming more and more popular across the country as a way to engage students in science. Chris said he took his team to a statewide robotics competition in Dallas. "Guess what happened?" he asked. "Our kids won first place. . . . Guess who won second?" I couldn't figure out where this was headed. Then he said, "Your alma mater. Highland Park High School." Chris's students had outperformed the students at my alma mater, the highly regarded public school that serves the residents of the privileged community where I grew up.

Chris's story tells us that we can in our lifetime see the day when children growing up in low-income communities have the same opportunities as those who grow up in high-income communities. Knowing that our vision is within reach, my colleagues and I are more determined than ever to do whatever it takes to get there.

An Invitation

I want to extend a personal invitation to all the college seniors and recent college graduates who are reading this book. I hope you will consider becoming part of this movement. We'll reach our vision only if you—our nation's future leaders—believe it's important and commit yourselves to the effort. If you're interested in becoming a corps member, please contact us at joinourcorps@teachforamerica.org or 1-800-832-1230.

We also hope to hear from all those interested in becoming involved in or supporting Teach For America in any way. For more information, please visit www.teachforamerica.org, e-mail me directly at wendyk@teachforamerica.org, or contact Teach For America at:

Teach For America
315 W. 36th Street, 6th Floor
New York, NY 10018
Tel: 212-279-2080

PublicAffairs is a publishing house founded in 1997. It is a tribute to the standards, values, and flair of three persons who have served as mentors to countless reporters, writers, editors, and book people of all kinds, including me.

I. F. Stone, proprietor of *I. F. Stone's Weekly*, combined a commitment to the First Amendment with entrepreneurial zeal and reporting skill and became one of the great independent journalists in American history. At the age of eighty, Izzy published *The Trial of Socrates*, which was a national bestseller. He wrote the book after he taught himself ancient Greek.

Benjamin C. Bradlee was for nearly thirty years the charismatic editorial leader of *The Washington Post*. It was Ben who gave the *Post* the range and courage to pursue such historic issues as Watergate. He supported his reporters with a tenacity that made them fearless, and it is no accident that so many became authors of influential, best-selling books.

Robert L. Bernstein, the chief executive of Random House for more than a quarter century, guided one of the nation's premier publishing houses. Bob was personally responsible for many books of political dissent and argument that challenged tyranny around the globe. He is also the founder and was the longtime chair of Human Rights Watch, one of the most respected human rights organizations in the world.

· · ·

For fifty years, the banner of Public Affairs Press was carried by its owner Morris B. Schnapper, who published Gandhi, Nasser, Toynbee, Truman, and about 1,500 other authors. In 1983 Schnapper was described by *The Washington Post* as "a redoubtable gadfly." His legacy will endure in the books to come.

Peter Osnos, *Publisher*